Battle, Capture
& Escape

Corporal Edwards

Battle, Capture & Escape

The Experiences of a
Canadian Light Infantryman
During the Great War

George Pearson

Battle, Capture & Escape: the Experiences of a Canadian Light Infantryman During the Great War
by George Pearson

Originally published in 1918 unbder the title
The Escape of a Princess Pat
Being the Full Account of the Capture and Fifteen Months' Imprisonment of Corporal Edwards, of the Princess Patricia's Canadian Light Infantry, and His Final Escape from Germany into Holland

Leonaur is an imprint of Oakpast Ltd

Text in this form and material original to this edition
copyright © 2008 Oakpast Ltd

ISBN: 978-1-84677-600-7 (hardcover)
ISBN: 978-1-84677-599-4 (softcover)

http://www.leonaur.com

Publisher's Notes

The opinions expressed in this book are those of the author and are not necessarily those of the publisher.

Contents

Preface	9
Polygon Wood	11
The Fourth of May	15
Corporal Edwards Takes Up the Tale	17
Major Gault Comes Back	22
The Last Stand of the Princess Pats	25
Prisoners	32
Pulling the Leg of a German General	40
The Princess Patricia's German Uncle	46
The German Red Cross and the Canadian Wounded	50
Acorn Coffee and Shadow Soup	53
The Way They Have at Giessen	57
The Escape	68
The Traitor at Vehnmoor	74
Four Miles to Freedom	79
In Napoleon's Footsteps	91
The Third Escape	101
The Fight in the Wood	112
Safe Across the Border	117
Holland at Last	123
It's a Way They Have in the Army	128
Author's Note	134
The Evidence in the Case	135

To the memory of our comrades who fell. . . .
This book is dedicated

Preface

In order to remove all question of doubt in the mind of the reader it might perhaps be well to state here that the facts as given are the *bona fide* experiences of Corporal Edwards, Number 39, Number One Company, P. P. C. L. I., and as such were subjected to the closest scrutiny both by the author and others before it was deemed advisable to give the account to the public. In particular great pains were taken to do full justice to all enemy individuals who figure in the story. Recognizing the seriousness of the charges implied by the recital, all those concerned with it are extremely anxious that the correctness of the account should constitute its chief value: In short the intention has been to make of the story a readable history.

The main facts—having to do with the destruction of the regiment on the eighth of May, 1915, the identity and activities of the individuals mentioned and the more important of the later happenings, including the final escape into Holland—are matters of official record and as such have frequently been mentioned in the official dispatches. The more personal details are based on the recollections of Corporal Edwards' retentive mind, aided by his very unusual powers of observation and the rough diary which he managed to retain possession of during his later adventures. For the events preceding the capture of Corporal Edwards on the eighth of May the author has relied upon his own recollections; as he too had the honour of having been "an original Patricia."

G. P.

CHAPTER 1

Polygon Wood

The Princess Patricias had lain in Polygon Wood since the twentieth of April, mid-way between the sanguinary struggles of St. Julien and Hill 60, spectators of both. Although subjected to constant alarm we had had a comparatively quiet time of it, with casualties that had only varied from five to fifty-odd each day.

By day and night the gun-fire of both battles had beat back upon us in great waves of sound. There were times when we had donned our water soaked handkerchiefs for the gas that always threatened but never came, so that the expectation might have shaken less steady troops. Quick on the heels of the first news of the gas the women of Britain, their tears scalding their needles, with one accord had laboured, sans rest, sans sleep, sans everything, so that shortly there had poured in to us here a steady stream of gauze pads for mouth and nostril. For the protection of our lungs against the poison of the gas they were at least better than the filthy rags we called handkerchiefs. We wore their gifts and in spirit bowed to the donors, as I think all still do. We soaked them with the foul water of the near-by graves and kept them always at our side, ready to tie on at each fresh alarm.

Once there had come word in a special army order of the day: "Our Belgian agent reports that all enemy troops on this front have been directed to enter their trenches tonight with fixed bayonets. All units are enjoined to exercise the closest watch on their front; the troops will stand to from the first appearance of darkness, with each man at his post prepared for all eventualities. Sleep will not be permitted under any circumstances."

The consequence had been that that night had been one of nervous expectation of an attack which did not materialise. We always carried fixed bayonets in the trenches but the Germans were better equipped with loopholes, as they were with most other things, and were forced to leave their bayonets off their rifles in order to avoid any danger of the latter sticking in their metal shields when needed in a hurry, to say nothing of the added attention they would draw in their exposed and stationary position at the mouth of a loophole. The "Stand-to" had come as a distinct relief that morning.

And always there had been the glowering fires of a score of villages. The greater mass of burning Ypres stood up amongst them like the warning finger of God. Occasionally the roaring burst of an ammunition dump flared up into a volcano of fiery sound. The earth under our feet trembled in convulsive shudders from a cannonade so vast that no one sound could be picked out of it and the walls of dug-outs slid in, burying sleeping men. But like the promise of God there came to us in every interval of quietness, as always, the full-throated song of many birds.

Our forces consisted of the French who held the left corner of the Ypres salient, then the Canadian division in the centre, next the 28th Division of the regular British Army and then our own, the 27th, with Hill 60 on our right flank. The enemy attacked both at Hill 60 and at the line of the Canadian Division and the French, and we held on to the horse-shoe shaped line until the last possible moment when one more shake of the tree would have thrown us like ripe fruit into the German lap.

So near had the converging German forces approached to one another that the weakened battery behind our own trenches had been at the last, turned around the other way and fired in the opposite direction without a shift in its own position. For our own protection we had nothing. And later still these and all other guns left us to seek new positions in the rear so that only we of the infantry remained.

Daily there had come orders to "Stand-to" in full marching order, to evacuate; at which all ranks expostulated angrily. And then perhaps another order—to stick it another day; at which we cheered and slapped one another boisterously on the back so that the stolid Germans over yonder must have wondered, knowing what they did of our desperate situation.

But the dreaded order came at last and was confirmed, so that under protest and like the beaten men that we knew we were not, we slunk away under cover of darkness on the night of the third of May to trenches three miles in the rear, and with us went the troops on ten more miles of British front.

The movement as executed was in reality a feat of no mean importance on the part of the higher command. Faced by an overwhelmingly superior force, our badly depleted three divisions had barely escaped being bagged in the net of which the enemy had all but drawn the noose in a strategic surrounding movement.

In detail, the movement had consisted of withdrawing under cover of darkness with all that we could carry of our trench material, both to prevent it falling into hostile hands and equally to strengthen our new position. A small rearguard of fifteen men to the regiment had held our front for the few hours necessary for us to "shake down" in the new position. Their task was to remain behind and to give a continuous rapid-fire from as many different spots as possible in a given time, thereby keeping up the illusion of a heavily manned trench. Then, they too had faded quietly away, following us.

Our new trenches were three miles behind those we had just evacuated in Polygon Wood. Zillebeke lay just to the left and beyond that, Hooge. We were in the open, with Bellewaarde Wood and Lake behind us.

We continued to face vastly superior forces. To make matters worse the trenches were assuredly a mockery of their kind and there was even less of adequate support than before. And at that the drafts arrived each day—if they were lucky enough to break through the curtains of fire with which the enemy covered our rear for that very purpose, as well as for the further one of curtailing the arrival of all necessary supplies of food and ammunition.

Every camp and hospital from Ypres to Rouen and the sea

and from Land's End to John O' Groat was combed and scraped for every eligible casualty, every overconfident office holder of a "cushy" job, and in short, for all those who could by hook or crook hold a rifle to help stem this threatening tide. And in our own lot, even those wasteful luxuries, the petted officers' servants were amongst us, doing fighting duty for the first time, so that we almost welcomed the desperate occasion which furnished so rare and sweet a sight.

CHAPTER 2

The Fourth of May

We suffered cruelly on the Fourth. The dawn had discovered two long lines of men, madly digging in plain sight of one another. There was no firing except that one little storm when the stronger light had shown our rear guard ridiculously tangled up with a screen of German scouts so that some of each were nearer to foe than to friend and so had foes on either side. They shot at one another. Some of us in our excitement shot at both, scarce able to distinguish one from the other. Others amongst us strove to knock their rifles up. And the Germans in their trenches shot too. Both of us of the main bodies continued to respect the tacit truce imposed by the conditions under which we found ourselves, insofar as we ourselves were concerned, and fired only at the poor fellows in between.

As for them, I fear the absurd nature of their tragic plight excited more of wonder than of concern. They merged into hedges and ditches swallowed them. Their case was only one incident of many, and what became of them I have never heard, except that Lieutenant Lane who commanded our rear guard was with us on the Eighth, so I presume that some must have crawled up to us that night and so saved themselves for the moment. Anything else would have been a great pity for so brave a squad.

The digging continued until the better equipped Germans had finished their task; when they sought their holes with one accord, an example which we as quickly followed.

This was at nine o'clock on the morning of the fourth of May. From then on until dusk the intensity of a furious all-day bombardment by every known variety of projectile had been broken only at intervals to allow of the nearer approach of the enemy's attacking infantry. The worst was the enfilade fire of two batteries on our right which with six-inch high explosive shells tore our front line to fragments so that we were glad indeed to see the night come. Only once had ours replied, one gun only. That was early in the morning. It barked feebly, twice, but drew so fierce a German fire that it was forever silenced.

Some infantry attacks followed but were beaten off. Only a weak half of the battalion was in the front line trench. The remainder were in Bellewaarde Wood, the outer fringe of which was a bare one hundred yards behind the front line. They were fairly comfortable in pine bough huts which were, however, with some of their occupants, badly smashed by shell fire that day.

The outcome was that although all attacks were beaten off, our losses were well on to two hundred men, most of whom were accounted for in the more exposed front line.

The order had been that we were to hold this front for several days more although the regiment had been in the trenches since April the 20th, and, except for a march back to Ypres from Polygon Wood, since early April. But after such a smashing blow on men who were already thoroughly exhausted, the plan was changed and our line was taken over by the King's Shropshire Light Infantry, the "Shrops" we called them, a sister regiment in our brigade, the 80th.

CHAPTER 3

Corporal Edwards Takes Up the Tale

It was on this day that I rejoined the regiment. I had been wounded in the foot at St. Eloi in February and had come up in a draft fresh from hospital and had lain in the supports at the huts all of the Fourth.

The survivors of the front line fire joined those at the huts shortly after nightfall. They were stupid from shell fire, too dazed to talk. I saw one man wandering in half circles, talking to himself—and with a heavy pack on. There were others in worse plight; so there was no help for him.

Myself, I was too much engrossed in a search for my comrade Woods to bother with other men less dear, however much I might sympathise with them.

He and I had been "mates" since Toronto days, had made good cheer together in the hot August days of mobilisation at Ottawa and had rubbed mess tins together under the starry sky at Levis before the great Armada had taken us to English camps and other scenes.

It was he who had fetched me out of danger at St. Eloi. And now it was my turn. They told me he was somewhere on a stretcher.

I searched them all. I struck matches—and was met by querulous curses; I knelt by the side of the dying; I inquired of those wounded who still could walk, but find him I could not. It appears that a new and heavy moustache had helped to hide him from me. I was in great distress, but in the fullness of time and when our small circles had run their route, I discovered him in Toronto.

The word was that we were to go to Vlamertinghe, where the Zeppelins had bombed us in our huts. It lay well below threatened Ypres.

We of Number One Company passed Bellewaarde Lake, with its old dug-outs and its smells, and struck off across the fields, the better to avoid the heavy barrage fire which made all movement of troops difficult beyond words. We reached the railroad up and down which in quieter times the battalion had been wont to march to and fro to the Polygon Wood trenches.

The fire became heavier here and the going was rough so that what with the burden of packs which seemed to weigh a ton and all other things; we moved in a mass, as sheep do. When slung rifles jostled packs, good friends cursed one another both loud and long. This was trench nerves.

Shortly, we ran into a solid wall of barrage fire. The officer commanding the company halted us. We were for pushing on to that rest each aching bone and muscle, each tight-stretched and shell-dazed nerve fairly screamed aloud for. But he was adamant. We cursed him. He pretended not to hear. This also was trench nerves.

It was growing late. The star shells became fewer. The searchlights ceased altogether. In half an hour those keen eyes in distant trees and steeples would have marked us down—and what good then the agony of this all-night march? Better to have been killed back there in Bellewaarde. We were still a good two miles from Ypres town.

The officer literally drove us back over the way we had come. His orders had anticipated this eventuality so that rather than force the passage of the barrage fire, merely for a rest, we should rest here where no rest was to be had. Undoubtedly, if we had been "going up" it would have been different. We should have gone on—no fire would have stopped us.

The half hour limit brought us to a murky daylight and an old and sloppy support trench which bordered the track and

British wounded waiting for transportation to a dressing station

The Princess Patricias in billets at Westoutre, Belgium—on top of wagon in foreground is "knife-rest" type of wire entanglements

into which we flung ourselves, to lay in the water in a dull stupor that was neither sleep nor honest waking.

Later, when the rations had been "dished out" we bestirred ourselves and so found or dug queer coffin-shaped shelves in either wall. Out of courtesy we called them dug-outs.

I do not remember that any one spoke much of the dead.

The rain stopped and for a time the unaccustomed sun came out. We drove stakes in the walls above our coffins, hunted sandbags and hung them and spare equipment over the open face and then crawled back into the water which, as usual, was already forming in the hollows that our hips made where we lay. Until noon there was little heard but the thick breathing of weary men. Occasionally one tossed and shouted blasphemous warnings anent imaginary and bursting shells; whereat those within hearing whined in a tired and hopeless anger, and, if close by, kicked him. Trench nerves.

All day the fire of many guns sprayed us. Near by, the well defined emplacement of one of our own batteries inevitably drew to the entire vicinity a heavy fire so that one shell broke fair amongst our sleeping men.

CHAPTER 4

Major Gault Comes Back

That was on the fifth. In the afternoon young Park came to us. He was the Commanding Officer's orderly. There was down on his face but he was full of all that strange wisdom of a trench-man who had experienced the bitter hardships and the heartbreaking losses of a winter in the cursed salient of St. Eloi, by Shelley Farm and The Mound of Death. But just now this infant of the trenches had the round eyes of a startled child, which in him meant mad excitement.

"The C.O.'s hit."

The word slid up the trench: "The C.O.'s hit."

"Strike me! Cawn't this bleedin' regiment keep a bleedin' Colonel——? That makes two of them!"

"How did it happen?"

"What the devil are we goin' to do?"

"Who says so?"

"The second in six weeks!"

"Parkie."

"By——! This mob's in a Hell of a fix, Bo'."

Park was leaning on his rifle, trench fashion. "Oh, dry up. You give me a pain."

And then he launched his thunderbolt, "Gault's back."

The chorus of despair became one of wild delight.

"We're jake!"

"He'll see us through."

"Where is he?"

"How's his arm?"

"The son-of-a-gun! Couldn't keep him away, could they?"

"No fear. Not 'im. Bloody well wanted to be wiv 'is bleedin' boys, 'e did. 'E ain't bloody well goin' to do 'is bloody solderin' in a 'cushy' job in Blighty—like some of 'em. Not after rysin' us. Do it wiv 'is bloody self like a man; an' that's wot 'e is."

The speaker glared accusingly; but his declaration agreed too well with what all thought for any one to take exception to it.

The new Commanding Officer had been wounded at St. Eloi on March 1st and this was our first intimation of his return.

Park took up his tale. "He's over there with the C.O. now," and switching: "Shell splinter got him in the eye. Guess it's gone and maybe the other one too."

"By——!" he burst out passionately: "I hope it don't. He's been damn good to me—and to you fellows too," he added fiercely, while his lower lip quivered.

I think all stared anywhere but at Park, in a curious embarrassment.

"Got it goin' from one trench to another to see about the rations comin' up instead of stayin' in like a 'dug-out *wallah.*' Got out on top of the ground, walked across an' stopped one," he added bitterly.

A considerable draft of "old boys," ruddy of face and fresh from hospital, together with some more new men reached us that night. We "went up" again with the dusk of the following night and "took over" our previous trenches in front of Bellewaarde Wood.

We were told that the Shropshires had been rather badly cut up in the interval of their occupation by a further course of intense bombardment and some fierce infantry fighting. Nevertheless, the trenches had been put into much better shape since our earlier occupancy of them, so that what with our work that night they were by the morning of the seventh in fairly good shape.

The night was not unusual in any way. There was the regular amount of shelling, of star shells, of machine gun and rifle fire, and of course, casualties. Those we always had, be it ever so quiet.

Even the morning "Stand-to" with that mysterious dread of unknown dangers that it invariably brought gave us nothing worse than an hour of chilly waiting—and later, the smoke of the Germans' cooking fires.

There were none for us. It was as simple as algebra. Smoke attracted undue artillery attention—the Germans had artillery; we had not. They had fires; we had not.

The day rolled by smoothly enough. Except for the fresh graves and a certain number of unburied dead the small-pox appearance of the shell-pitted ground about might have been thought to have been of ancient origin; so filled with water were the shell holes and so large had they grown as a result of the constant sloughing in of their sodden banks.

During all these days the German fire on the salient at large had continued as fiercely as before but had spared us its severest trials.

The night of the seventh passed to all outward appearance pretty much in the same manner as the preceding one.

CHAPTER 5

The Last Stand of the Princess Pats

It seemed as though I had just stepped off my whack of sentry go for my group when a kick in the ribs apprised me that it was "Stand-to." I rubbed my eyes, swore and rose to my feet. Such was the narrowness of the trench that the movement put me at my post at the parapet, where in common with my mates, I fell to scanning the top for the first signs of day and the Germans.

The latter lay on the other side of the ravine from us as they had since the Fourth, except for such times as they had assaulted our position. The smoke of Ypres and all the close-packed villages of a thickly populated countryside rose sullenly on every hand.

Over everything there hung the pallor of the mist-ridden Flemish morning, deadly quiet, as was usual at that time of the trench day when the tenseness of the all-night vigil was just merging into the relieving daylight.

At half past six that stillness was punctuated by a single shell, which broke barely in our rear. And then the ball commenced— the most intense bombardment we had yet experienced. Most of the fire came from the batteries in concealed positions on our right, whence, as on the fourth, they poured in a very destructive enfilade fire which swept up and down the length of the trench like the stream of a hose, making it a shambles. Each burst of high-explosive shells, each terrible pulsation of the atmosphere, if it missed the body, seemed to rend the very brain, or else stupefied it.

The general result was beyond any poor words of mine. All spoken language is totally inadequate to describe the shocks and horrors of an intense bombardment. It is not that man himself lacks the imaginative gift of words but that he has not the word tools with which to work. They do not exist. Each attempt to describe becomes near effrontery and demands its own separate apology.

In addition, kind Nature draws a veil for him over so much of all the worst of it that many details are spared his later recollection. He remembers only the indescribable confusion and the bursting claps of near-by flame, as foul in colour and as ill of smell as an addled egg. He knows only that the acid of the high-explosive gas eats into the tissue of his brain and lungs, destroying with other things, most memories of the shelling.

Overhead an aeroplane buzzed. We could even descry the figures of the pilot and his observer, the latter signalling. No gun of ours answered. The dead and dying lay all about and none could attend them: A rifle was a rifle.

This continued for an hour, at the end of which time we poked our heads up and saw their infantry coming on in columns of mobs, and some of them also very prettily in the open order we had ourselves been taught. Every field and hedge spewed them up. We stood, head and shoulders exposed above the ragged parapet, giving them "Rapid-fire." They had no stomach for that and retired to their holes, leaving many dead and grievously wounded.

It was at this time that we saw the troops on our flanks falling back in orderly fashion. I called that fact to the attention of Lieutenant Lane, who was the only officer left in our vicinity. He said that the last word he had received was to hang on.

This we proceeded to do, and so, we are told, did the others. We learned later that the battalion roll call that night showed a strength of one hundred and fifty men out of the six hundred and thirty-five who had answered "Present" twenty-four hours earlier. And the official records of the Canadian Eye Witness, Lord Beaverbrook, then Sir Max Aitken, as given in *Canada in Flanders*, state that "Those who survive and the friends of those who have died may draw solace from the thought that never in the history of arms have soldiers more valiantly sustained the gift and trust of a Lady," referring to the Colour which had been worked for and presented to us by the Princess Patricia, daughter of His Royal Highness the Duke of Connaught, then Governor-General of Canada.

We were on the apex of the line and were now unsupported on either side. It was about this time, I believe, that a small detachment of the King's Shropshire Light Infantry, a sister regiment in our brigade, fetched to the companies in our rear twenty boxes of badly needed ammunition and reinforced the Princess Patricias.

Following the beating off of their infantry attack the Germans gave us a short breathing spell until their machine guns had been trained on our parapet and a school of light field guns dragged up into place. The aeroplane came out again, dropping to within three hundred feet of our trench, and with tiny jets of varicoloured smoke bombs, directed the terribly accurate fire of the enemy guns, already so close to, but so well insured against any harm from us that they attempted no concealment. And the big guns on the right completed the devastation.

This continued for another half hour, at the end of which time there remained intact only one small traverse in the trench, which owed its existence to the fragment of chicken wire that held its sides up. The remainder was absolutely wiped out. This time there was no rapid fire, nor even any looking over the top to see if the enemy were coming on. Instead, the Germans fairly combed the parapet with their machine guns. Each indication of curiosity from us drew forth from them such a stream of fire that the top of the parapet spat forth a steady shower of flying mud, and, which made it impossible for us to defend ourselves properly, even had there been enough of us left to do so.

The rest was chaos, a bit of pure hell. Men struggling, buried alive and looking at us for the aid they would not ask for. Soldiers all. And the Germans now pouring in in waves from all sides, and especially from our unprotected flanks and rear, hindered only by the desultory rifle fire of our two weakened companies in the support trenches. We were receiving rifle fire from four directions and bayonet thrusts from the Germans on the parapet. Mowed down like sheep. And as they came on they trampled our dead and bayoneted our wounded.

The machine-gun crew had gone under to a man, doing their best to the last. I think Sergeant Whitehead went with them, too; at least he was near there a short time before, and I never saw him or any of the gun crew again. The only living soul near that spot was Royston, dragging himself out from under a pile of debris and covered with mud and blood, his face horribly swollen to twice its normal size, blinded for the moment.

To quote *Canada in Flanders* again:

> At this time the bombardment recommenced with great intensity. The German bombardment had been so heavy since May 4th that a wood which the Regiment had used in part for cover was completely demolished. The range of our machine-guns was taken with extreme precision. All, without exception, were buried. Those who served them behaved with the most admirable coolness and gallantry. Two were dug out, mounted and used again. One was actually disinterred three times and kept in action till a shell annihilated the whole section. Corporal Dover stuck to his gun throughout and, although wounded, continued to discharge his duties with as much coolness as if on parade. In the explosion that ended his ill-fated gun, he lost a leg and an arm, and was completely buried in the debris. Conscious or unconscious, he lay there in that condition until dusk, when he crawled out of all that was left of the obliterated trench and moaned for help. Two of his comrades sprang from the support trench—by this time the fire trench—and succeeded in carrying in his mangled and bleeding body. But as all that remained of this brave soldier was being lowered into the trench a bullet put an end to his sufferings. No bullet could put an end to his glory.

George Easton was firing with me at the gray mass of the oncoming horde. "My rifle's jammed!" he cried.

"Take mine." And I stooped to get one from a casualty underfoot. But a moment later, as I fired from the parapet, my bayonet was broken off by a German bullet. I shouted wildly to Cosh to toss me one from near by.

Just then the main body of the Germans swarmed into the end of the trench.

Of this Lord Beaverbrook says: "At this moment the Germans made their third and last attack. It was arrested by rifle fire, although some individuals penetrated into the fire trench on the right. At this point all the Princess Patricias had been killed, so that this part of the trench was actually tenantless. Those who established a footing were few in number, and they were gradually dislodged; and so the third and last attack was routed as successfully as those which had preceded it."

His conclusion that we had all been killed was justifiable even though, fortunately for me, it was an erroneous one. So I am glad for other motives than those of mere courtesy to be able here to set him right.

Bugler Lee shouted to me: "I'm shot through the leg." A couple of us seized him, planning to go down to where the communication trench had once been. But he stopped us, saying: "It's no good, boys. It's a dead end! They're killing us."

Cosh swore. "Don't give up, kid! We'll beat the———yet!" A German standing a few yards away raised his rifle and blew his head off. Young Brown broke down at this—they had just done in his wounded pal: "Oh, look! Look what they've done to Davie," and fell to weeping. And with that another put the muzzle of his rifle against the boy's head and pulled the trigger.

Young Cox from Winnipeg put his hands above his head at the order. His captor placed the muzzle of his rifle squarely against the palm and blew it off. There remained only a bloody and broken mass dangling from the wrist.

I saw a man who had come up in the draft with me on the 4th, rolling around in the death agony, tossing his head loosely about in the wild pain of it, his pallid face a white mark in the muck underfoot. A burly German reached the spot and without hesitation plunged his saw-edged bayonet through the throat.

German prisoners after a successful Canadian attack, bringing wounded men down a communication trench

Close by another wounded man was struggling feebly under a pile of earth, his legs projecting so that only the convulsive heaving of the loose earth indicated that a man was dying underneath. Another German observed that too, and shoved his bayonet through the mud and held it savagely there until all was quiet.

This I did not see, but another did and told me of it afterward. Sergeant Phillpots had been shot through the jaw so that he went to his knees as a bullock does at the slaughtering. He supported himself waveringly by his hands. The blood poured from him so that he was all but fainting with the loss of it.

A big German stood over him.

Phillpots looked up: "Play the game! Play the game!" he muttered weakly.

The German coolly put a round through his head.

I was still without a bayonet, and seeing these things, said to Easton: "We'd better beat it."

He swore again. "Yes, they're murdering us. No use stopping here. Come on!"

And just then he, too, dropped. I thought him dead. There was no use in my stopping to share his fate or worse. It was now every man for himself. At a later date we met in England.

The other half of the regiment lay in support two hundred yards away in Bellewaarde Wood and in front of the château and lake of that name, where my draft had lain on the fourth. I made a dash for it. What with the mud and the many shell holes, the going was bad. I was indistinctly aware of a great deal of promiscuous shooting at me, but most distinctly of one German who shot at me about ten times in as many yards and from quite close range. I saw I could not make it. I flung myself into a Johnson hole, and as soon as I had caught my breath, scrambled out again and raced for the trench I had just left. I was by this time unarmed, having flung my rifle away to further my flight, notwithstanding which another German shot at me as I went toward him.

As I landed in the trench an angry voice shouted something I could not understand. And I scrambled to my feet in time to see a German sullenly lower his rifle from the level of my body at the command of a big black-bearded officer.

CHAPTER 6

Prisoners

The Germans were by this time in full possession of this slice of trench, and for the next few minutes the officer was kept busy pulling his men off their victims. Like slavering dogs they were. He did not have his lambs any too well in hand, however. O.B. Taylor, a lovable character in Number One Company, came to his end here. The Germans ordered him and Hookie Walker to go back down the trench. He had no sooner turned to do so than a German shot him from behind and from quite close, so that it blew the groin completely out, making a terrible hole. We could not tie up so bad a wound and he bled to death. Hookie Walker remained with him to the last, five hours later, when he said: "I'm going to sleep boys," and did so. Fortunately, he did not suffer. And all the others except young Cox were equally fortunate, since they were murdered outright.

Taylor's was the most calculated of all the murders we had witnessed and outdid even those of the wounded because the excitement of the fight was two hours old and he was doing the bidding of his captors at the time. The killing of those who resisted was of course quite in order. Why he was killed while Walker was left unharmed and at his side to the last we did not know and could only credit to a whimsy of our captors. No punishment was visited upon his murderer or upon any of them so far as we were able to learn.

Upon my later return to Canada I found that Taylor's sister there had received a letter from a German officer enclosing a letter addressed to her which had been found on her brother's body, together with three war medals and a Masonic ring. The latter was the key to the incident since the officer also claimed to have been a Mason. In his letter this officer said that her brother had met a soldier's death!

Some said that our friendly officer was not a German but an Irishman. I doubted that but it may have been so, for it was true that his speech contained no trace of the accent which is usually associated with a German's English speech. His was that of an English gentleman. And to him we undoubtedly owed our wretched lives that day.

I in particular have good cause to be grateful. A German, all of six foot four, who swung a tremendously broad headsman's axe with a curved blade, tried several times to get at me. Each time the officer stopped him. Still he persisted. He apparently saw no one else and kept his eye fastened on me with deadly intention in it. He pushed aside the others, Prussians and prisoners alike; he whirled the shining blade high above a face lit up with savage exultation, terrible to see, and which reflected the sensual revelling of his heated brain in the bloody orgy ahead. As I followed the incredibly rapid motions of the blade, my blood turned to water. My limbs refused to act and my mind travelled back over the years to a little Scottish village where I had been used to sit in the dark corners of the shoemaker's shop, listening to him and others of the old 2nd Gordons recount their terrible tales of the hill men on the march to Kandahar with "Bobs." And now I felt that same tremendous sensation of fear which used to send me trembling to my childish pallet in the croft, peering fearfully through the darkness for the oiled body of a naked Pathan with his corkscrew *kris*. Terror swept over me like a springtime flood. He saw no one else. His eye fastened on me in crudest hate. But as he stood over me with feet spread wide and the circle of his axe's swing broadening for the finale, the thread of rabbit-like mesmerism broke and I sprang nimbly aside as the blade buried itself deep in the mud wall I had been cowering against. I endeavoured to dodge him by putting some of my fellow prisoners between us. No use. He followed me, shoving and cursing his way among them, swinging his axe. My hair stood on end and

I felt rather critical of their much-vaunted Prussian discipline. Another endeavoured to bayonet Charlie Scarfe. The officer at last stopped them both.

Our captors belonged to the Twenty-first Prussian Regiment and were, so far as we knew, the first of their kind we had been up against, all previous comers on our front having been Bavarians and latterly of the army group of Prince Ruprecht of Bavaria—"Rupie," we called him. They wore the baggy grey clothes and clumsy looking leather top boots of the German infantryman. The spiked *pickelhauben* was conspicuous by its absence and was, we well knew, a thing only of billets and of "swank" parades. In its place was the soft pancake trench cap with its small coloured button in the front.

The enemy were armed for the most part with pioneers' bayonets, as well adapted by reason of their saw edges for sticking flesh and blood as for sawing wood; and, if for the former, an unnecessarily cruel weapon, since it was bound to stick in the body and badly lacerate it internally in the withdrawal; especially if given a twist.

The trench front had been about-faced since its change of ownership and the Germans were already casting our dead out of the shattered trench, both in front and behind, and in many cases using them to stop the gaps in the parapet; so that they now received the bullets of their erstwhile comrades.

We were ordered up and out at the back of the parapet and then made to lie there. The German artillery had ceased. We had none. Odd shots from the remnant of our fellows still hanging on in the supports continued to come over, but none of us were hit. In all probability, they withheld their fire when they saw what was afoot. Some German snipers in a farmhouse at the rear were less considerate, but fortunately failed to hit us.

Later we were ordered to take our equipment off and those who had coats, to shed them. We did not see the latter again and missed them horribly in the rain of that day. Two of the Prussians "frisked" us for our tobacco, cigarettes, knives and other valuables.

This was in bitter contrast to our own treatment of prisoners under similar conditions. True, we had always searched them but had invariably returned those little trinkets and comforts which to a soldier are so important. And I think our men had always showered them with food and tobacco.

We were then marched to the rear, with the exception of one, who, by permission of the officer, remained with the dying Taylor.

There were ten of us all told. I have only heard of a few others who were captured that day. Roberts is still in Germany and Todeschi has been exchanged and is now in Toronto. The latter lay with a boy of the machine-gun crew for a couple of days in a dug-out, both badly wounded. A German stumbled on to them. They pleaded for water. The German said, "I'll give you water" and bayoneted the boy as he lay. He raised his weapon so that the blood of his comrade dripped on Todeschi's face.

"All right," Todeschi cried in German, "kill me too, but first give me water, you——"

The German lowered his rifle in amazement: "What, you *schwein*, you speak the good German? Where did you learn it?"

"In your schools. For Christ's sake—give me water—and kill me."

"What! You live with us and then do this? *Schwein!*"

"All right, I will give you water and I will not kill you; just to show you how well we can treat a prisoner."

Todeschi was then taken to the field dressing station where according to his own account his mangled leg was amputated without the use of any anaesthetic. But that may have been because in such a time of stress they had none. Later he was exchanged.

I met Scott in the prison camp a few days later and he told his tale. It appears that in the confusion of the earlier fighting he had become separated from the regiment, became lost and eventually floundered into an English battalion. He reported to the officer commanding the trench and told his story. The officer had no idea where the Patricias lay and so ordered Scott to remain with them until such time as an inquiry might establish the whereabouts of his regiment.

They were captured, but under less exciting circumstances than occurred in our own case. And the Germans had word that there was a Canadian amongst these English troops. It was one of the first things mentioned. They did not say how they had acquired their information, but shouted out a request for the man to stand forth. When no one complied, they questioned each man separately, asking him if he was a Canadian or knew aught of one in that trench.

They all lied: "No." The Germans were so certain that they again went over each man in turn, examining him.

Scott was at the end of the line. He began to cut the Canadian buttons off his coat and to remove his badges. Several men near by assisted and replaced them with such of their own as they could spare; each man perhaps contributing a button. They had no thread nor time to use it if they had, so tacked the buttons into place by all manner of makeshifts, such as broken ends of matches thrust through holes punched in the cloth; anything to hold the buttons in place and tide the hunted Scott over the inspection. He passed. The Germans were quite furious.

Scott and his companions could only guess at the cause of this strange conduct, but presumed that the Canadian was wanted for special treatment of an unfavourable, if not of a final nature.

To return to our own case:

About the middle of the afternoon we were herded by our guards into a shallow depression a short distance in the rear of the trench and there told to lie down. The officer and his men returned to the trench. Until we were taken back to the trench at six we were continually sniped at by the Germans in the captured trench. We had no recourse but to make ourselves as small as possible, which we did. And whether owing to the fact that the hollow we were lying in prevented our being actually within the range of the enemy vision, or whether they were merely playing cat and mouse with us, I do not know, but none were hit. Young Cox suffered stoically. His mangled hand had become badly fouled with dirt and filth, and the ragged bones protruded through the broken flesh. So, in a quiet interval between the sniping periods we hurriedly sawed the shattered stump of his hand off with our clasp knives and bound it up as best we could. It was not a nice task, for him nor us, but he did not so much as grunt during the operation. The nearest he came to complaining was when he asked me to let him lay his hand across my body to ease it, at the same time remarking: "I guess when they get us to Germany they'll let us write, and I'll be able to write mother and then she'll not know I've lost my hand." He was a most valiant and faithful soldier.

The perpetual rain and mist peculiar to that low-lying land added to our wretched condition and increased the pain of the wounds that most of us suffered from.

At six o'clock our guards returned and curtly ordered us to our feet. We were taken back to the trench, where our officer friend had us searched again. Here for the first time my two corporal's stripes were noticed and a mild excitement ensued. *"Korporal! Korporal!"* they exclaimed and crowded up the better to inspect me and verify the report, and jabbering *"Ja! Ja!"* Apparently a captured corporal was a rarity. Strangely enough, they paid little or no attention to the sergeant of our party, although he had the three stripes of his rank up.

As I happened to be in the lead of our party and the first to enter the trench, I was the first man searched and so had to await the examination of the others. Worn out by the events of the day and the wound I had received early in the morning from a shell fragment, I fell asleep against the wall of the trench where I sat.

I was awakened by a poke in the ribs from Scarfe. "Time to shift, mate."

I rose to my feet and, following the instructions of the officer, led the way along the trench. The Germans had already, with their usual industry, gotten the trench into some sort of shape again, with the parapet shifted over to the other side and facing Bellewaarde Wood. And everywhere along its length I noticed the bodies of our dead built into it to replace sandbags while others lay on the *parados* at the rear.

It was not nice. The faces of men we had known and had called comrade looked at us now in ghastly disarray from odd sections of both walls. Already they were taking a brick-like shape from the weight of the filled bags on top of them. In places the legs and arms protruded, brushing us as we passed. However, this was war and quite ethical.

Naturally we had to crowd by the other occupants of the trench. And each took a poke at us as we went by, some with their bayonets, saying: *"Verdamnt Engländer"* and: *"Engländer Schwein,"*—pigs of English. Also quite a number of them spoke English after a fashion. There was in these men none of the soldier's usual tolerance or good-natured pity for an enemy who had fought well and had then succumbed to the fortunes of war. Instead, a blind and vicious rage which took no account of our helpless condition.

They cuffed us, they buffeted us, they pricked us cruelly with their saw bayonets and then laughed and sneered as we flinched and dodged awkwardly aside. Then they cursed us.

Shortly, we were led into the presence of a man whom I shall remember if I live to be a hundred. He wore glasses and on his upper lip there bloomed such a dainty moustache as is affected by "Little Willie" as Tommy calls the German Crown Prince. He had the eye of a rat. It snapped so cruel a hate that one's blood stopped.

He seized me by the right shoulder with his left hand: "You Corporal! You Corporal!" as though that fact of itself condemned me, and at the same time tugging at his holster until he found his revolver, which he placed against my temple. Then and there I fervently prayed that he would pull the trigger and end it all. I was fed up. The all-day bombardment, the last terrible slaughter of helpless men, the rain and cold, combining with the pain of the raw wound in my side, had gotten on my nerves. With the revolver still at my head I turned to Scarfe: "They're going to do us in, Charlie. I only hope they'll do it proper. None of that bayonet stuff. Bullets for me." Already the Prussians were crowding round us threateningly again, with their saw-edged bayonets ready, some fixed in the rifle, others clasped short, like daggers, for such a butchering as they had had earlier in the afternoon, when I had been so nearly axed.

"Might as well kill us outright as scare us to death," complained Scarfe bitterly.

Nevertheless our hearts leaped when a moment later our mysterious black officer friend hove in sight. Life is sweet.

He asked them what they did with us. The tableau answered for itself before the words had left his lips. And then we had to listen to our fate discussed in language and gesture so eloquent and so fraught with terrible importance to us that our sensitized minds could miss no smallest point of each fine shade of cruel meaning.

"Little Willie" thought it scarce worth their while to bother with so small a bag; that it would not be worth the trouble to send a miserable ten of *Verdamnt Engländer* back to the Fatherland—Better to kill them like the swine they were.

Our blood froze to hear the man and to see the poison of that rat soul of his exuding from his every pore, in every gesture and in each fresh inflection of his rasping voice. And all his men shouted their fierce approval and shook in our faces their bloody butcher's bayonets. It was a bitter draught. If they had killed us then it would have had to have been done in most cold blood, exceeding even the murder of Taylor in planned brutality. He at least had not known that it was coming and had not felt this insane fear which we now experienced and which made us wonder how they would do it. Would each have to watch the other's end? And would it be done by bullet or by bayonet? We greatly feared it would be the latter. We pictured ourselves held down as hogs are—our throats slit——!

The dark officer thought otherwise and minced no words in the saying. Our hearts leapt out to him warmly, in gratitude.

He sharply ordered them to desist, at which they slunk sullenly away, as hungry dogs do from a bone.

I felt an uncomfortable physical sensation and ran my hand uneasily beneath my shirt. I was covered with a fine sweat.

CHAPTER 7

Pulling the Leg of a German General

We were then escorted under heavy guard out over the fields in the rear, past the nearby farmhouse, which was simply filled with snipers. The latter, however, did not shoot at us, presumably because they might have hit some of our numerous guards. We seemed to be working right through the heart of the German Army. Everywhere the troops were massed. Along the road they lay in solid formation on both sides. If we had had artillery to play on them now they would have suffered tremendous losses. The whole countryside presented a living target. All the way they shouted *"Schwein"* and taunted us in both languages. Every shell-hole, farmhouse, hut, dugout and old trench on the three-mile stretch between the Front and Polygon Wood contributed its quota.

The regiment had evacuated Polygon Wood on the night of the third. Across the old trail our fatigue parties had tramped new ones in the mud, up past Regent Street, Leicester Square and Piccadilly. We passed them all.

We were marched over to the little settlement of pine-bough huts which the regiment had previously taken over from the French. The men with me greeted them like old friends. Here was the Sniper's Hut, there the Commanding Officer's. This was the hut in which the brave Joe Waldron had "gone West," that on the site of one where fourteen of "ours" had stopped a shell while they slept. Memories submerged us and made us weak. Even the guiding rope that our men had used to hold themselves to the trail of nights still held its place for groping German hands.

Beside it lay the fragments of the French signboards, jocular advertisements of mud baths for trench fever, the *hôtel* this and the *maison* that. One of my companions pointed to a larger hut which he said our fellows had called the Hotel Cecil. The board was missing now. And no German signboard took its place. Their wit did not run in so richly innocent a channel.

The huts lay just off the race track in front of the ruined château, buried deep in the remnants of what had once been the beautiful park of a large country estate. These huts were now the German headquarters.

There was as much English as German talked there that day. Everywhere there was cooking going on, mostly in portable camp kitchens.

As we came to a halt one big fellow smoking a pipe observed nonchalantly: "You fellows are lucky. Our orders were to take no Canadian prisoners."

The man was so casual, so utterly matter-of-fact and there was about his remark so simple an air of directness and of finality that there was no escaping his sincerity, unduly interested though we were.

Another officer said *"Engländer?"*

The big fellow said *"Kanadien."* The other raised his brows and shoulders: "Uhh!"

A younger officer came up: "Never mind, boys: Your turn today. Might be mine tomorrow." Turning to the others, he too said: *"Engländer?"*

"No! Canadian."

"Oh!" And he appeared to be pleasantly surprised. He asked me for a souvenir and pointed to the brass Canada shoulder straps and the red cloth "P. P. C. L. I.'s" on the shoulders of the others. But I had already shoved my few trinkets down my puttees while lying back of the trench that afternoon. Scarfe, however, gave up his "Canada" straps.

The young officer gave him in return a carved nut with sil-

WOUNDED CANADIANS RECEIVING FIRST AID IN A
SUPPORT TRENCH AFTER AN ATTACK

ver filigree work and gave another man a silver crucifix for the bronze maple leaves from the collar of his tunic. And, more important still, he gave us all a cigarette, while he had a sergeant give us coffee.

That, the cigarette, was I think much the best of anything we received then or for some time to come. Since the bombardment and our wounding, our nerves had fairly ached for the sedative which, good, bad or indifferent, would steady the quivering harp strings of our nerves. And a cigarette did that.

The headquarters staff appeared on the scene. They wanted information, just as ours would have done under similar circumstances, but these took a different method to acquire it. As before, in the trench, they selected me for the spokesman. The senior officer, a general apparently, addressed me: "How many troops are there in front of our attack?"

I lied: "I don't know."

He shook a threatening finger at me. "I'll tell you this, my man: We have a pretty good idea of how many troops lay behind you and if in any particular you endeavour to lead us astray it will go very hard with all of you. Now answer my question!" His English was good.

I cogitated. It would not do to tell him the terrible truth. That was certain. So I took a chance. "Three divisions." He appeared to be satisfied. The fact was, there were none behind us. We were utterly without supporting troops.

"And Kitchener's Army? How many of them are there here?"

"Why, they haven't even come over yet, sir."

"Don't tell me that: I know better. They've been out here for months."

"But they haven't," I persisted. I told the truth this time.

"Yes," he shouted angrily.

"No," I flung back.

"Well, how many of them are there?"

The division yarn had gone down well. And perhaps I was slightly heated. My spirit ran ahead of my judgment. "Five and a half to seven million," I said.

He exploded. And called me everything but a soldier. I could not help but reflect that I had overdone it a bit. And I certainly thought that I was "for it" then and there.

To make matters worse he asked the others and they, profiting by my mistake and following the lead of the first man questioned, put Kitchener's army at four and a half million; which was only a trifle of four million out. So I determined to be reasonable. When he came to me again I confirmed the latter figure, explaining my earlier statement by my lack of exact knowledge. And so that particular storm blew over.

The general came back to me again. "You Canadians thought this was going to be a picnic, didn't you?" He was very sarcastic.

"No, we didn't, sir."

"Well, you thought it was going to be a walk through to Berlin, didn't you?"

"Why, no. We thought it was the other way about, sir," I ventured.

He shifted: "Well, what do you think of us anyhow?"

"Your artillery was all right but your infantry was no good." I began to feel shaky again. However, he took that calmly enough.

"Oh! So our infantry was no good."

"We could have held them all right, sir."

He ruminated on that a moment, rumbled in his throat and abruptly changed the subject, in an unpleasant fashion, however.

"You're the fellows we want to get hold of. You cut the throats of our wounded."

I denied it and we argued back and forth over that for several minutes, and very heatedly. He referred to St. Julien and said that this thing had occurred there. I said and quite truthfully that we had not been at St. Julien, that we were in the Imperial and not the Canadian Army and had been spectators in near-by trenches of the St. Julien affair. I even went into some detail to explain that we were a special corps of old soldiers who, not being able to rejoin their old regiments, had at the outbreak of war formed one of their own and had been accepted as such and sent to France months ahead of the Canadian contingent. I added that I myself had just rejoined the regiment, having got my "Blighty" in March at St. Eloi and as proof of my other statements I further volunteered that I was one of the 2nd Gordons and after the South African War had gone to Canada where I had finished my reserve several years since.

He listened but was plainly unconvinced. Another officer broke in: "I can explain it, sir. These men were in the 80th Brigade and the 27th Division. Colonel Farquhar was their Commanding Officer and Captain Buller took command when Colonel Farquhar was killed." We stared at one another in amazement, for it was all quite true.

This finished that examination. We did not tell them that Colonel Buller had been blinded a few days before and had been succeeded by that Major Hamilton Gault who had been so largely instrumental in raising us.

None of our wounds had received the slightest attention. Cox in particular suffered cruelly but refused to whimper. Royston's head was swollen to the size of a water bucket and he was in great pain. We left them here and never saw them again. Cox died two weeks later of a blood poisoning which was the combined result of our rough surgery and the wanton neglect of our captors. I do not think he was ever able to write his mother as he wished. At least she wrote me later for information. There was no need of his dying even though it might have been necessary to have amputated his arm higher up. Royston was exchanged to Switzerland and recovered from his wounds except for the loss of an eye.

Chapter 8

The Princess Patricia's German Uncle

We were marched to Roulers, which we reached well after dark. A considerable crowd of soldiers and civilians awaited our coming. The Belgian women and children congregated in front of the church while we waited to be let in, and threw us apples and cigarettes. The *uhlans* and infantrymen rushed them with the flat side of their swords and the butts of their muskets; and mistreated them. They knocked one old woman down quite close to where I stood. So we had to do without and were not even permitted to pick up the gifts that lay at our feet, much less the old woman.

The church had been used as a stable quite recently and the stone-flagged floor was deep with the decayed straw and accumulated filth of men and horses. We lay down in it and got what rest we could for the remainder of the night. There were about one hundred and fifty prisoners in all—Shropshires, Cheshires, King's Royal Rifles and other British regiments—all from our division and mostly from our brigade. Other small parties continued to come in during the night, but there were no more P.P.'s. In the morning a large tub of water was carried in and each man was given a bit of black bread and a slice of raw fat bacon. The latter was salty and so thoroughly unappetizing that I cannot recall that any one ate his ration, for in spite of the fact that we had been twenty-four hours without food, we were so upset by the experiences we had undergone, so shattered by shell fire and lack of rest that we were perhaps inclined to be more critical of our food than normal men would have been.

Shortly afterward a high German officer came in with his staff. He was a stout and well-built man of middle age or over, typically German in his general characteristics but not half bad looking. His uniform was covered with braid and medals. Every one paid him the utmost deference. He stopped in the middle of the room.

"Are there any Canadians here?"

I stepped forward. "Yes, sir."

"I mean the Princess Patricia's Canadians."

"Yes, sir. I am. And here's some more of them," and I pointed at the prostrate figures of my companions, where they sprawled on the flagstones.

"Princess Patricia's Regiment?"

"Yes, sir."

"Well, the Princess Patricia is my niece—awfully nice girl. I hope it won't be long before I see her again."

I grinned: "Well, I hope it won't be long before I see her, too, sir."

The other fellows joined us, the straw and the smell of it still sticking to their clothes as they formed a little knot about the Prince and his staff.

The scene was incongruous, the smart uniforms of the immaculately kept staff officers contrasting strangely with our own unkempt foulness. We occupied the centre of the stage. Around us were grouped the men of our sister regiments, most of them lying on the floor in a dazed condition. There were few who came forward to listen. They were too tired, and to them at least, this was merely an incident—one of a thousand more important ones. Odd parts of clothes hung on the ornate images and decorations of the room. A German rifle hung by its sling from the patient neck of a life-sized Saviour, while further over, the vermin-infested shirt of a Britisher hung over the rounded breasts of a brooding Madonna, with the Infant in her lap.

At the door a small group of guards stood stiffly to a painful attention and continued so to do whilst royalty touched them with the shadow of its wings.

The Prince questioned us further and I told him that I had been on a guard of honour to the Princess when she had been a child and when her father, the Duke of Connaught had been the General Officer Commanding at Aldershot.

He laughed back at us and was altogether very friendly. "You'll go to a good camp and you'll be all right if you behave yourselves."

Scarfe shoved in his oar here, grousing in good British-soldier fashion: "I don't call it very good treatment when they steal the overcoats from wounded men."

"Who did that?" He was all steel, and I saw a change come over the officers of the staff.

"The chaps that took us prisoners," said Scarfe.

"What regiment were they?" The Prince glanced at an aide, who hastily drew out a notebook and began to take down our replies.

"The 21st Prussians, sir."

"Do you know the men?"

"Their faces but not their names."

"Of what rank was the officer in charge?"

We did not know, but thought him a company officer of the rank of captain perhaps. He asked for other particulars which we gave to the best of our knowledge.

"I'll attend to that," he said. However, we heard no more of it. We refrained from complaining about the actual ill-treatment and indignities we had been subjected to, the murder of our unoffending comrades, or the lack of attention to our wounds, as we rightly judged that we should only have earned the enmity of our guards.

"May I have your cap badge?" the Prince asked, decently enough.

I lied brazenly: "Sorry, sir; I've lost mine."

The fact was I had shoved it down under my puttees while lying back of the trench the previous afternoon.

Scarfe said: "You can have mine, sir."

He took it. "Thanks so much." He glanced at the aide again; rather sharply this time, I thought. The latter blushed and hastily extracted a wallet, from which he handed Scarfe a two-mark piece, equal to one and ten pence, or forty-four cents. He gave us his name before leaving, and my recollection is that it was something like Eitelbert. Evidently he was a brother of the Duchess of Connaught, whom we knew to have been a German princess whose brothers and other male relatives all enjoyed high commands among our foes.

CHAPTER 9

The German Red Cross and the Canadian Wounded

We remained in the fouled church all of that day and night and until the following morning. No more food appeared. We were marched down to the railroad under heavy escort, crowded into freight cars and locked in. The guards were distributed in cars of their own, alternating with ours. Our wounds remained unattended to.

At every station they thundered: "Come out, Canadians!" They lined us up in a row while a staff officer put the same questions to us in nearly every case. They were particularly interested in the quality of our rations and asked if it was not true that we were starving and if our pay had not been stopped. The guards invariably explained to the civilians that these were the Canadians who had cut the throats of the German wounded.

We did not know how to explain the prevalence of this impression. On the contrary, we were aware of the story of the crucifixion of three of the Canadian Division during Ypres. The tale had come smoking hot to our men in the Polygon Wood trenches during the great battle. It gave in great detail all the salient facts which were that after recapturing certain lost positions, the men of a certain regiment had discovered the body of one of their sergeants, together with those of two privates, crucified on the doors of a cowshed and a barn. German bayonets had been driven through their hands and feet and their contorted faces gave every appearance of their having died in great agony. This story was and is generally believed throughout all ranks of the Canadian Army. For its truth I cannot vouch.

We knew that our own men had never mistreated any prisoners and had in fact usually done quite the reverse. How far other regiments may have gone in retaliation for what was known as "The Crucifixion," it is impossible to say. That prisoners may have been killed is possible, for such things become an integral part of war once the enemy has so offended. But we could not believe that there had been any cutting of throats as that would imply a sheer cold-bloodedness that we could not stomach.

The mob surged around and reviled us, while the guards, in high good humour, translated their remarks, unless, as was frequently the case, they were made to the officials in English for our benefit. The other British soldiers were left in their cars.

Our wounded were getting very badly off by this time. It was impossible to avoid trampling on one another as the car was very dark at best and the one small window in the roof was closed as soon as we drew into a station. When taken out we were under heavy escort and were allowed no opportunity to clean up the accumulated filth of the car. We suffered terribly for food and water, and some of the wounds began to turn, so that what with exhaustion and all, we grew very weak.

At one station the guards took us out and made us line up to watch them eat of a hearty repast which the Red Cross women had just brought them. And we were very hungry. When, we too, asked for food they said: *"Nix! Nix!"* The crowds met us at every station and included women of all classes, who called us *Engländer Schwein* and who at no time gave us the slightest assistance, but, instead, devoted themselves to the guard.

Other men told us later that Red Cross women had spat in their drinking water and in their food. There was no opportunity for this in our case as we did not receive any of either.

We did not receive any food during this trip, which lasted from the morning of one day until the night of the next. We had gone since the day of our capture on the coffee received at headquarters in Polygon Wood and the single issue of bread, water and bacon received in the church, the latter of which we could not eat; a total of three days and nights on that one issue of rations.

We pulled into Giessen at eleven, the night of May tenth. The citizens made a Roman holiday of the occasion and the entire population turned out to see the *Engländer Schwein*. There was a guard for every prisoner, and two lines of fixed bayonets. The mob surged around, heaping on us insults and blows; particularly the women. With hate in their eyes, they spat on us. We had to take that or the bayonet. These were the acts not only of the rabble, but also of the people of good appearance and address.

One very well-dressed woman rushed up. Under other circumstances I should have judged her to have been a gentlewoman. She shrieked invectives at us as she forced her way through the crowd. *"Schwein!"* she screamed, and struck at the man next me. He snapped his shoulders back as a soldier does at attention. Then, drawing deep from the very bottom of her lungs, she spat the mass full in his face. The muscles of his face twitched painfully but he held his eyes to the front and stared past his tormentor, seeing other things.

CHAPTER 10

Acorn Coffee and Shadow Soup

We had a mile-and-a-half march to the prison camp. Those who were past walking were put in street cars and sent to the *laager*, where upon our arrival we were shoved into huts for the night, supperless, of course. This was our introduction to the prison camp of Giessen.

The next morning we each received three-quarters of a pint of acorn coffee, so called, horrible-tasting stuff; and a loaf of black bread—half potatoes and half rye—weighing two hundred and fifty grams, or a little more than half a pound, among five men. This allowed a piece about three by three by four inches to each man for the day's ration. The coffee consisted of acorns and four pounds of burned barley boiled in one hundred gallons of water. There was no sugar or milk. My curiosity led me later to get this and other recipes from the fat French cook.

All that day and for several following, official and guards were busy numbering and renumbering us and assigning us to our companies. They were hopelessly German about it, and did it so many times and very thoroughly. There were twelve thousand men in the camp and eight hundred in the *laager*. The majority were Russian and French with a fairish sprinkling of Belgians. There were perhaps six hundred British in the entire camp. The various nationalities were mixed up and each section given a hut very similar to those American and British troops occupy in their own countries. A number of smaller camps in the neighbouring districts were governed from this central one.

For dinner we had shadow soup, so named for obvious reasons. The recipe in my diary reads: "For eight hundred men, two hundred gallons of water, one small bag of potatoes and one packet of herbs."

To make matters worse the vegetables issued at this camp were in a decayed condition and continued to come to us so.

Another staple dinner ration was ham soup. This was the usual two hundred gallons of water boiled with ten pounds of ham rinds, ten pounds of cabbage and twenty pounds of potatoes. The ham rind had hair on it but we used to fish for it at that and considered ourselves lucky to get a piece. Oatmeal soup, another meal, consisted of two hundred gallons of water, two pounds of currants and fifty pounds of oatmeal; chestnut soup, two hundred gallons of water, one hundred pounds of whole chestnuts and ten pounds of potatoes. It was a horrible concoction and my diary has: "To be served hot and thrown out."

Meat soup was two hundred gallons of water, ten pounds of meat, one small bag of potatoes and ten pounds of vegetables. This was the most nutritious of the lot. Unfortunately for us, the small portion of meat and most of the potatoes were given to the French, both because the cook and all his assistants were Frenchmen and because the authorities willed it so.

This was usually managed without any apparent unfairness by serving the British first and the French last, with the result that the one received a tin full of hot water that was too weak to run out, while the Frenchmen's spoons stood to attention in the thicker mess they found in the bottom. This, with other things, contributed to make bad blood between the two races. A great show was made of stirring up the mess, but it was a pure farce.

Rice soup consisted of two hundred gallons of water, fifty pounds of rice, twenty pounds of potatoes and one pound of currants; bean soup, two hundred gallons of water, fifty pounds of beans, and twenty pounds of potatoes; pork soup, two hundred gallons of water, ten pounds of pork and fifty pounds of potatoes. Porridge was made of two hundred gallons of water, fifteen pounds of oatmeal and two pounds of barley. The diary states: "To be served hot as a drink."

Once in two months a ration of sausage was dished out. For

Wednesday 8

Soups in Giessen P.O.W
Camp. Recipes

1 Shadow Soup
For 800 men
200 Gallons water, 1 small bag
potatoes, 1 packet herbs.

Thursday 9

2 Oatmeal Soup
200 Gallons water 50 lbs oatmeal 2 lbs currants

3 Meat Soup
200 Gallons water 10 lbs meat
1 small bag potatoes 10 lbs
vegetables

Friday 10

4 Chestnut Soup

200 Gallons water 100 lbs
Chestnuts

RECIPES FROM CORPORAL EDWARD'S DIARY

breakfast once a week there was one pint of acorn coffee without sugar or milk and one and a half square inches of Limburger cheese. To quote from the diary: "Before serving, open all windows and doors. Then send for the Russians to take it away."

The Germans discriminated against the British prisoners. When there was any disagreeable duty; the cry went up for *"der Engländer."* The much-sought-for cookhouse jobs all went to the French, who waxed fat in consequence. No Britisher was ever allowed near the cookhouse. The French had for the most part been there for some time, and, their country lying so close by; they were receiving parcels. We were not, and this made the food problem a very serious one for us. Their supplies were received through Switzerland which was the one anchor to windward for so many of us in this and other respects.

At first the French used to give us a certain amount of their own food, but eventually ceased to do so. Most of them worked down in the town daily and could "square" the guard long enough to buy tobacco at twenty-five pfennigs—or two and a half pence—a package, which they sold to us later at eighty pfennigs—until we got on to their profiteering.

CHAPTER 11

The Way They Have at Giessen

Except for the starving, as I look back now, Giessen was not such a bad camp as such places go. At least it was the best that we were to know. The discipline, of course, was fairly severe, but on the other hand the Commandant did not trouble us a great deal. The petty annoyances were harder to endure. Frequently we would get the *"Raus!"* at half-hour intervals by day or night; *"Raus* out!" *"Raus* in!" and so on.

We never knew what our tormentors wanted but supposed it to be a systematic attempt to break our spirit and our nerve by the simple expedient of habitually interfering with our sleep so that we would become like the Russians. They were mostly utterly broken in spirit and had the air of beaten dogs, so that they cringed and fawned to their masters.

The least punishment meted out for the most trifling offense was three days' cells. Some got ten years for refusing to work in munitions and steel factories, particularly British and Canadians.

There are large numbers of both who are today serving out sentences of from eighteen months to ten years in the military fortresses of Germany under circumstances of the greatest cruelty.

The so-called courts-martial were mockeries of trials. The culprit was simply marched up to the orderly room, received his sentence and marched away again. He was allowed no defence worthy of the name.

Some of the King's Own Yorkshire Light Infantry were "warned" for work in a munitions factory. When the time came around they were taken away but refused to work and so they were knocked about quite a bit. One was shot in the leg and another bayoneted through the hip, and all were sent back to camp, where they were awarded six weeks in the punishment camp, known as the strafe barracks.

This was a long hut in which were two rows of stools a few paces apart. The *Raus* blew for the culprits at five-thirty. At six they were marched to the hut and made to sit down in two rows facing one another, at attention—that is, body rigid, head thrown well back, chest out, hands held stiffly at the sides and eyes straight to the front—for two hours! Meanwhile the sentries marched up and down the lane, watching for any relaxation or levity. If so much as a face was pulled at a twinkling eye across the way, another day's strafing was added to the penalty. At the end of the two hours one hour's rest was allowed, during which the prisoners could walk about in the hut but could not lie down! This continued all day until "Lights out." For six weeks. No mail, parcels, writing or exercise was permitted the prisoners during that time, and the already scanty rations were cut.

During good behaviour we were allowed two post cards and two letters a month, with nine lines to the former and thirteen to the page of the latter. No more, no less. Each letter had four pages of the small, private-letter size. The name and address counted as a line. Mine was *Kriegsgefingenenlaager, Kompagnie No. 6, Barackue No. A.* The writing had to be big and easily read and, in the letters, on four sides of the paper. No complaint or discussion of the war was permitted. Fully one-half of those written were returned for infringements, or fancied ones, of these rules. Sometimes when the censor was irritated they were merely chucked into the fire. And as they had also to pass the English censor it is no wonder that many families wondered why their men did not write.

We were there for three months before our parcels began to arrive. We considered ourselves lucky if we received six out of ten sent, and with half the contents of the six intact. In the larger camps the chances of receipt were better. The small camps were merely units attached to and governed by the larger ones, which handled the mail before giving it to the authorities at the smaller ones.

Thus, a man who was "attached" to Giessen camp, although perhaps one hundred miles away from it, had to submit to the additional delay and chance of loss and theft included in the censoring of the parcel at Giessen as well as at the actual place of his confinement.

This doubled the chances of fault-finding and of theft. Knowing this to be true, I most earnestly recommend the sending of parcels. True, a large proportion of them are not received, but those that are represent the one salvation of the prisoner-of-war in German hands. So terribly true is this that when we began to receive parcels at irregular intervals, we used regularly to acknowledge to our friends the receipt of parcels which we had never received. This was the low cunning developed by our treatment. If advised that a parcel of tea, sugar or other luxuries had been sent and it did not appear after weeks of patient waiting, we knew that we should never see that parcel. Nevertheless, we usually wrote and thanked the donor and acknowledged the receipt, fearful otherwise that he or she should say: "What's the use?" and send no more. And we were not allowed to tell the truth—that it had been stolen.

The first three months of our stay at Giessen were probably the worst of all, including as they did the transition period to this life. It seemed then a hell on earth. The slow starvation was the worst. Once, in desperation, I gave a Frenchman my good boots for his old ones and two and a half marks, and then gave sixty pfennigs of this to the French cook for a bread ration. Again, in going down the hut one day, I espied a flat French loaf cut into four pieces, drying on the window sill. Seizing one piece, I tucked it under my tunic and passed on before the loss was discovered. Some of the British could be seen at times picking over the sour refuse in the barrels. This amused the Germans very much. We endeavoured to get cookhouse jobs for the pickings to be had, but could not do so. At a later date, when the Canadian Red Cross, Lady Farquhar, Mrs. Hamilton Gault and our families were sending us packages regularly, we made out all right.

Some English societies were in the habit of sending books,

music and games to the prisoners but none of these ever reached the group with whom I associated, even before our later actions put us quite beyond the German pale.

The appeal for Casement and the Irish Brigade was made to us. A number of prisoners were taken apart and the matter broached privately to them. Pamphlets on the freeing of Ireland were also distributed. I did not see any one go over, and an Irishman who was detailed with another Canadian and myself on a brickyard fatigue said that they had recruited only forty in the camp. The whole thing turned out to be a failure.

There were twelve of us all told on that brickyard job. Three or four shovelled clay into the mixing machine, two more filled the little car which two others pushed along the track of the narrow-gauge railroad. We were guarded by four civilian Germans of some home defence corps, all of whom laboured with us. The two trammers used to start the car, hop on the brake behind and let it run of its own momentum down the incline to the edge of the bank where it would be checked for dumping. Sometimes we forgot to brake the car so that it would ricochet on in a flying leap off the end of the track, and so on over the dump. The guards would rage and swear but could prove nothing so long as our fellows did not get too raw and do this too frequently.

One day we shovellers decided to add to the gaiety of nations. While one attracted the guards' attention elsewhere we slipped a chunk of steel into the mess. There was a grinding crash, and a large cogwheel tore its way through the roof. In a moment, the air was full of machinery and German words. It was a proper wreck. The guards ran around gesticulating angrily, tearing their hair and threatening us, while we endeavoured to look surprised. It is reasonable to suppose that we were unsuccessful, for we were hustled back to camp and drew five days' cells each from the Commandant. There was no trial. He merely sentenced us.

United States Ambassador Gerard only came to Giessen once in my time there, and that was while I was off at one of the detached camps, so I had no opportunity of observing the result.

We knew very little of what was going on in the outside world. The guards were not allowed to converse with us, and if one was known to speak English he was removed. However, they were more or less curious about us so that a certain amount of clandestine conversation occurred. Some were certain that they were going to win the war. Others said: "England has too much money. Germany will never win." They used frequently to gather the Russians, Belgians and French together and lecture them on England's sins. They said that England was letting them do all the fighting, bleeding them white of their men and treasure so as to come out at the end of the war with the balance of power necessary for her plan of retaining Constantinople and the Cinque Ports of France. Many were convinced, and this did not add to the pleasantness of our lot.

The notorious *Continental Times* was circulated amongst us freely in both French and English editions. It regularly gave us a most appalling list of German victories and it specialised in abuse of the English. We counted up in one month a total of two million prisoners captured by the Germans on all fronts.

As I have said, Giessen was the best camp of all, barring the starvation. But the discipline there was merciless. The *laager* was enclosed by a high wire fence which we were forbidden to approach within four feet of. A Russian sergeant overstepped that mark one day to shout something to a friend in an adjoining *laager*. The sentry shouted at him. He either failed to hear or did not understand. The sentry killed him without hesitation.

A Belgian started over one day with some leftover soup which he purposed giving to the Russians. The sentry would not let him pass. He went back and told his mate. The latter, a kindly little fellow, thinking that the sentry had not understood the nature of the mission, decided to try himself. The sentry stopped him. He attempted to argue. The sentry pushed him roughly back. He struck the German. The latter dropped him with a blow on the head, and while he lay unconscious shoved the bayonet into him. It was done quite coolly and methodically, without heat. He was promoted for it. We were told that he had done a good thing and that we should get the same if we did not behave.

A Canadian who was forced to work in a munitions plant and whose task included the replacing of waste in the wheel boxes of cars enjoyed himself for a while, lifting the greasy waste out and replacing it with sand. He got ten years for that.

The German in charge of our *laager* hated the *verdamnt Engländer* and lost no opportunity of bulldozing and threatening us. One of the Canadians who had been in the American Navy was unusually truculent. The German purposely bunted him one day. "Don't do that again!" The German repeated the act. The sailor jolted him in the jaw so that he went to dreamland for fifteen minutes. The prisoner was taken to the guardroom and we never heard his ultimate fate, but at the ruling rate he was lucky if he got off with ten years.

It is men like this to whom our Government and people owe such a debt as may be paid only in a small degree by our insistence after the war that they be given their liberty. A greater glory is theirs than that of the soldier. They wrought amongst a world of foes, knowing their certain punishment, but daring it rather than assist that foe's efforts against their country.

One day we were told that we must be inoculated in the arm against typhoid. We thought nothing of that. But the next day men began to gather in groups so that the guards shouted roughly at them, bidding them not to mutter and whisper so.

Where the word came from I know not. It may have emanated in the fears of some active imagination on the chance and truthful word of a guard, flung in derision at some desperate man, or in a kindlier mood and in warning. The word was that we were to be inoculated with the germs of consumption. I understand that it appeared also in the papers at home. It seemed horrible beyond words to us. The idea appeared crazy but was equally on a par with the events we witnessed daily. Myself, I planned to take no chances; if it were humanly possible.

We were all ordered to parade for the inoculation. I hid myself with a few others and so escaped the operation. Nothing was said so I could only suppose that they failed to check us up as it was not in keeping with the German character as

Fellow prisoners at Giessen, from left to right: a Cheshire Regiment man, a Siberian Russian, an East Yorkshire Light Infantryman and a Gordon Highlander

Fellow prisoners at Giessen, three Highlanders and a Yorkshire Light Infantryman

we had come to know it to miss any opportunity of corrective punishment even though the inoculation had been for our own good.

It is true that some of the men so inoculated fell prey to consumption. On the other hand one of them had had a well defined case of it before, and it was almost certain that the living conditions prevailing amongst us would insure the appearance of the disease so that we had no proof that any man was so inoculated. Some of the men so affected were sent to Switzerland for the benefit of the mountain air through an arrangement made by the Red Cross with the Swiss authorities.

One of our guards was subject to fits and habitually ran amuck amongst us, abusing some of the prisoners in a painful fashion. We made complaint of this through the proper channels, for which crime the officer in charge stopped our fires and other privileges for the time being.

Most of the men wore prison uniforms or in some cases, suits sent from England which were altered by the authorities to conform to their regulations. These required that if one was not in a distinctive and enemy uniform that broad stripes of bright coloured cloth be set into the seam of the trousers; not sewed on, but into the goods. A large diamond shaped piece or else a square of such cloth was set into the breast and back of the tunic. I preferred my uniform, dilapidated though it was. We were permitted the choice, probably less out of kindness than because of the saving involved.

There was a big simple giant of a Russian here who was badly sprung at the knees. He had been forced to work during the winter in an underground railway station near Berlin. He had had no shoes and had stood in the water for weeks, digging. He was very badly crippled in consequence.

Some four hundred Russians came to us after the fall of Warsaw. They were mostly wounded and all rotten. On the three months' march to Giessen the wounded had received absolutely no attention other than their own. Here we had a crazy German doctor, a mediocre French one and Canadian orderlies. If an Englishman went to the hospital for treatment it was "Vick!"—

Get out. These Russians were treated similarly. The French fared better. One big, fine-looking Russian, with a filthy mass of rags wound round his arm, reported for attention. They unwound the rag and his arm dropped off. He died, with five others, that afternoon, and God only knows how many more on the trip they had just finished.

They were buried in a piano case, together. Usually they were placed in packing cases. We asked for a flag with which to cover them as soldiers should be. They asked what that was for and there it ended.

Another Russian had a foul arm which leaked badly so that it was not only painful to him but offensive to the rest of us. Nothing was done for him.

They were all thoroughly cowed, as are dogs that have been ill-treated. And they jumped to it when a German spoke—excepting two of their officers, who refused to take down their epaulets when ordered to do so. We did not learn how they fared. These were the only captive officers of any nationality whom we saw.

We became sick of the sight of one another as even the best of friends do under such abnormal conditions. For variety I often walked around the enclosure with a Russian. Neither of us had the faintest idea what the other said, but it was a change!

The monotony of the wire was terrible—and just outside it in the lane formed by the encircling set of wire, the dogs, with their tongues out, walked back and forth, eyeing us.

There was so little to talk about. We knew nothing and could only speculate on the outcome of the commonest events which came to us on the tongue of rumour or arose out of our own sad thoughts.

The authorities were not satisfied with our recognition—or lack of it—of their officers and took us out to practice saluting drill—a thing always detested by soldiers, especially veterans. The idea was to make us salute visiting German officers properly, in the German fashion and not in our own. Theirs consisted of saluting with the right hand only, with the left held stiffly straight at the side, while our way was to salute with the hand farthest from the officer, giving "Eyes left" or "Eyes right" as the case might be, and with the free hand swinging loosely with the stride.

So a school of us were led out to this. The very atmosphere was tense with sullen rebellion. The guards eyed us askance. The officer stood at the left awaiting us; beyond him and on the other side of the road, a post.

An *unteroffizier* ordered us to march by, one by one, to give the *Herr Offizier "Augen Links"* in the German fashion, and to the post, which represented another officer, an *"Augen Rechts"* when we should come to it.

"I'll see him in hell first," I muttered to the man next me. I was in the lead of the party. I shook with excitement and fear of I knew not what.

As the command rang out I stepped out with a swing, and with the action, decision came to me. As I approached the officer he drew up slightly and looked at me expectantly.

I gave him a stony stare, and passed on.

A few more steps and I reached the post. I pulled back my shoulders with a smart jerk, got my arms to swinging freely, snapped my head round so that my eyes caught the post squarely and swung my left hand up in a clean-cut parabola to "Eyes right," in good old regimental order.

A half dozen shocked sentries came up on the double. It was they who were excited now. I was master of myself and the situation. The *unteroffizier* ordered me to repeat and salute. I did so—literally. The officer was, to all outward appearances, the only other person there who remained unmoved. My ardour had cooled by this time, and his very silence seemed worse than the threats of the guard. Nor was I exactly in love with my self-appointed task. Nevertheless, I saw my mates watching me and inwardly applauding. I was ashamed to quit. I did it again. That won me another five days' cells.

CHAPTER 12

The Escape

Mervin Simmons of the 7th, and Frank Brumley of the 3rd Battalion, Canadian Expeditionary Force were planning to escape. Word of it leaked through to me. This added fuel to the fire of my own similar ambition. They, and I too, thought that it was not advisable for more than two to travel together. I began to look around for a partner. I "weighed up" all my comrades. It was unwise to broach the subject to too many of them. I bided my time until a certain man having dropped remarks which indicated certain sporting proclivities, I broached the subject to him. He was most enthusiastic. We decided on Switzerland as our objective and awaited only the opportunity to make a break.

There were few if any preparations to make. We were not yet receiving parcels and our allowance of food was so scanty that it was impossible to lay any by. We had a crude map of our own drawing. And that was our all.

In the interval we discussed ways and means of later travel and endeavoured to prepare our minds for all contingencies, even capture. We talked the matter over with Simmons and Brumley at every opportunity, so as to benefit also by their plans. This required caution so we were careful at all times that we should not be seen together; rather that we should even appear unfriendly. We developed the cunning of the oppressed. Once we even staged a wordy quarrel over some petty thing for the benefit of our guards and others of the prisoners whom we distrusted. At other times we foregathered in dim corners of our huts as though by chance. We conversed covertly from the corners of our mouths and without any movement of the lips, as convicts do. This avoidance of one another was made the easier because of the arrangement of the personnel of each hut. The various nationalities were pretty well split up in companies, presumably to prevent illicit co-operation and each company was separated from the others by the wire.

Our chance came at last. We were "warned" for a working party on a railroad grade near by. As compliance would enable us to get on the other side of the wire, we made no protest. This work was a part of the authorities' scheme of farming prisoners out to private individuals and corporations who required labour. In this case it was a railroad contractor. As a rule the contractors fed us better than the authorities, if for no other reason than to keep our working strength up.

We were marched out of the *laager* without any breakfast each morning to the work and there received a little sausage and a bit of bread for breakfast. At noon we received soup of a better quality than the camp stuff. It was cooked by a Russian Pole, a civilian; one of many who was living out in the town on parole. These had to report regularly to the authorities and had to remain in the local area.

We were on the job a week before things seemed favourable. We had only what we stood in, excepting the rough map, which was drawn from hearsay and our scanty knowledge of the country. We planned to travel at night, lay our course by the stars and perhaps walk to Switzerland in six weeks.

We worked all morning, grading on the railroad embankment. At noon we knocked off for soup and a rest. We were on the edge of a large wood. Some of the men flung themselves on the bank; others went to see if the soup was ready. A few went into the wood. The solitary guard was elsewhere. We said goodbye to the few who knew of our plans. They bade us God-speed and then we, too, faded into the recesses of the wood.

We had no sooner set foot in it than I noticed a curious change come over my companion. He said that it was a bad time, a bad place, found fault with everything and said that we should not go that day. However, we continued, half-heartedly on his part, to shove our way on into the wood. Occasionally he glanced fearfully over his shoulder and voiced querulous protests. I did not answer him. A little further on and he stopped. A dog was barking.

"There's too many dogs about, Edwards. And just look at all those houses." He pointed to where a village showed through the trees.

"Sure thing, there'll be houses thick like that all the way. It's our job to keep clear of them."

"Yes, but look at the people. There's bound to be lots of them where there's so many houses."

"Of course there are," I replied: "Germany's full of houses and people. That's no news. Come on."

"Oh! They'll see us sure, Edwards—and telegraph ahead all over the country. We haven't got any more show than a rabbit."

With that I lost patience and gave him a piece of my mind. We stood there, arguing it back and forth.

It was no use: He fell prey to his own fears; saw certain capture and a dreadful punishment. He conjured up all the dangers that an active imagination could envisage: Every bush was a German and every sound the occasion of a fresh alarm. He was like to ruin my own nerves with his petty panics.

It was in vain that I pleaded with him: He could not face the dangers that he saw ahead. The *laager* seemed to him, by comparison, a haven of refuge. When all else failed, I appealed to his pride. He had none. I warned him that we should meet with nothing but scorn from our comrades, excepting laughter, which was worse. I begged and pleaded with him to go on with me. No use. All his courage was foam and had settled back into dregs.

And so we returned. I was heart-broken. But there was no use in my going on alone. To travel by night we must sleep in the day time and that required that some one should always be on watch to avoid the chance travellers of the day—which was obviously impossible for any one who travelled alone.

We had been gone only an hour and a half and the guard was just beginning to look around for us. Otherwise we had not been missed nor seen, for the wood was a large one and we had not yet gotten out of its confines. The guard was too relieved to find us, when we stepped out of the wood and picked up our shovels, to do more than betray a purely personal annoyance. He asked where we had been and why we had remained for so long a time. We gave the obvious excuse. He was too well pleased at his own narrow escape from responsibility to be critical, so that the affair ended in so far as he or his kind were concerned. Which made what followed the harder to bear.

For it was not so with our own comrades. My prognostication had been a correct one. A few of them had known that we were going; some had bade us goodbye. They rested on their picks now and stared at us, lifting their eyebrows, with a knowing smile for one another and a half-sneer for us. My companion had already plumbed the depths of fear and so was now lost to all shame. Myself, I found it very hard. Soldiers have, outwardly at least, but little tenderness, except perhaps in bad times, and they showed none now. Nor mercy. The situation would have been ridiculous had it not been so utterly tragic—to have failed without trying! Edwards's escape became camp offal. We became the butt and the byword of the camp, so that I honestly regretted not having pushed on alone. I felt sure that the almost certain capture and more certain punishment would have been more bearable than this. There was nothing that I could say in my own defence except at the other man's expense—which would have been in questionable taste and would have been deemed the resort of a weakling. So I kept my counsel and brooded. The ignorance of the guards made the tragedy comic. It was very humiliating. I gritted my teeth and swore that I at any rate should go again in spite of their incredulous jeers. But it was all terribly discouraging and made me most despondent.

And that finished that trip to Switzerland.

A few days later Simmons and Brumley disappeared. There was no commotion. One day they were with us and the next—they were not. The guards said nothing and we feared to ask. I longed ardently to be with them.

In a few days the camp was thrown into a mild turmoil. The

poor fellows were escorted in under a heavy guard. And very dejected they looked too—in rags, very wet and evidently short of food, sleep and a shave. Nevertheless, I envied them.

They disappeared for a long time. We were told they got two weeks' cells and six weeks of sitting on the stools in strafe barracks. I remembered the Yorkshiremen and my envy was tempered.

I spent most of my time casting about for the means for a real escape. Quite aside from my natural desire for freedom I felt that my good name as a soldier was at stake. However, I waited for an opportunity to converse with Simmons and Brumley before doing anything as I felt that their experience might contain some useful hints for me.

They appeared at the end of two months, quite undismayed. They told me of what had happened to them and Simmons approached me on the subject of making another try of it with them. I readily consented. They were now convinced that three or four could make the attempt with a better chance of success than two men. I would have agreed to go an army! All I wanted was an opportunity to prove my mettle and retrieve my lost reputation.

They told me their story. It seems that they had been sent out as a working party to a near by farm. They were locked in the room as usual at nine o'clock that night after the day's work and then waited until they had heard the sentry pass by a couple of times on his rounds. The window was covered with barbed wire which they had no difficulty in removing. By morning they were well on the way to Switzerland. They figured that they, too, could do it in six weeks' of walking by night, laying their course by the stars. They had no money and were still in khaki.

They were four days' out and lying close in a small clump of bushes adjoining a field in which women were digging potatoes when a small boy stumbled on them. They knew they had been seen the day before and chose this exposed spot rather than the near-by wood, thinking that it was there the hue and cry would run. But he was a crafty little brat and pretended that he had not seen them. They were not certain whether he had or not and hesitated to give their position away by running for it.

The boy walked until he neared the women, when he broke

into a run and soon all gathered in a little knot, looking and pointing toward the fugitives. Some of the women broke away and evidently told some Bavarian soldiers who had been searching. The latter had already been firing into the woods to flush them out so that if the boy had not seen them the soldiers would in all likelihood have passed on, after searching the main wood.

It was just four o'clock with darkness still four hours off. Simmons and Brumley were unarmed. There was no use in running for it. So they surrendered with what grace they could. There was the usual *verdamning*, growling and prodding but no really bad treatment. For this they were sentenced to two weeks cells and six weeks of strafe barracks.

They had been much bothered by the lack of a compass on their trip; so when they finished their strafing and were once more allowed the privileges of the mail, Simmons took a chance and wrote on the inside of an envelope addressed to his brother in Canada: "Send a compass." He was not called up so we hoped that it had gone through.

CHAPTER 13

The Traitor at Vehnmoor

Giessen is in Hesse. Shortly after this we were all sent to Cellelaager in Hanover. This was the head camp of a series reserved for the punishment or the working of prisoners. Each unit retained the name of Cellelaager and received in addition a number, as Cellelaager 1, Cellelaager 2 and so on. There were grounds here providing a lot for football, and a theatre run by the prisoners, for which there was an entrance fee, and other like amusements. These, however, were only for those prisoners who were on good behaviour and who were employed there. As such they were denied such desperadoes as ourselves.

We remained there for two weeks and were then sent to the punishment camp known as Vehnmoor or Cellelaager 6. This was a good day's ride away and also in Hanover, fifteen kilometres from the big military town of Oldenburg. Here we were turned out to work on the moors with four hundred Russians, one hundred French and Belgians and two hundred British and Canadians. We were housed in one large hut built on a swamp and were continually wet. There were only two small stoves for the seven hundred men and we had only a few two pound syrup tins in which to cook. A poor quality of peat was our only fuel. As only five men could crowd round a stove at a time, one's chances were rather slim in the dense mob, every man-jack of whom was waiting to slip into the first vacant place that offered.

We slept in a row along the wall, with our heads to it. Overhead a broad shelf supported a similar row of men. Above them were the windows. At our feet and in the centre of the room, there was a two foot passage way and then another row of men, with two shelves housing two more layers of sleepers above them. Then another two foot passageway, the row of men on the floor against the other wall and the usual shelf full above them. The vermin were bad and presented a problem until we arranged with the Russians to take one end to themselves, the French and Belgians the middle and we the other end. By this means we British were able to institute precautionary measures amongst ourselves so that after feasting on the Russians and finishing up upon the French, our annoying friends usually turned about and went home again.

The swamp water was filthy, full of peat and only to be drunk in minute quantities at the bidding of an intolerable thirst. There was no other water to be had and we simply could not drink this. The Russians did, which meant another fatigue party to bury them. The only doctor was an old German, called so by courtesy; but he knew nothing of medicine. As a corporal, I was held responsible for twenty men. That implied mostly keeping track of the sick and I have seen nineteen of my twenty thus. But that made no difference. It was *"Raus!"* and out they came, sick or well.

Every morning an officer stood at the gate as we marched out to the moor, to take "Eyes right" and a salute, for no useful purpose that we could see except to belittle a British soldier's pride. As corporal I was supposed to give that command to my squad but rather than do so I took my stripes down, although that ended my immunity as a "non-com" from the labour of cutting peat. Others, I am sorry to say, were glad to put the stripes up and at times went beyond the necessities of the situation in enforcing their rule on their comrades. It was one of these who was found to be trading in and selling his packages to his less fortunate comrades and who was ostracized in consequence.

There were here at Vehnmoor, as there had been at Giessen, a certain few of our own men who traded on the misfortunes of their own comrades. This man was the worst of them all. He was a sergeant-major in a certain famous regiment of the line in the British Army. He was a fair sample of that worst type which the army system so often delegates authority to—and complains because that authority does not meet with the respect it should on the part of its victims.

He excelled in all the arts of the sycophant: The pleasure of the guards was his delight, their displeasure, his poignant grief. He assumed the authority of his rank with us, he reported the slightest of misdemeanours amongst us to the guards and was instrumental in having many punished. These and other things gave him and others of his kidney the run of the main grounds so that they could stretch their legs and have some variety in their lives. Such liberty was there for any man who would do as they did.

None of us were safe from these traitors. The sergeant major in particular, spied on us, reporting all criticisms of our guards and other things German. We raged. He had for his virtue a small room to himself in a corner of the hut. When parcels came from England, addressed to the senior non-commissioned officer of his regiment, for him to distribute; he called the guards in. Shortly they went out with their coats bulging suspiciously. We were then called to receive ours whilst he stood over, bullying us with all the abusive "chatter" which the British service so well teaches. And afterward we watched covertly, with all the cunning of the oppressed, and saw him receive other stealthy favours from the guards that were not within his arrangement with the Commandant.

So one of his own men who had a certain legal learning took down all these facts as I have recited them and calling us together, bade us sign our names in evidence of so foul a treachery. Which we gladly did. And it was and is the prayer of all that when the gates of the prison camps roll back this document will get to the War Office and there receive the attention it deserves.

My comrades in misfortune here told me of another such a man who had gone away just before my arrival at this camp. He, too, was a sergeant-major of a line regiment in the old army. I had known him in the old days in India. In his own regiment he was never known by his own name, but instead by this one:

"The dirty bad man." No one ever called him anything else when referring to him. That was his former record and this is what he did here to keep the memory of it green.

He was instrumental in having fixed on us one of the most terrible of army punishments. It appears that some time before one of our men had broken some petty rule of discipline and the Germans had asked the sergeant-major what the punishment was in our army for such a "crime," as all offences are termed in the army.

"Number One Field Punishment or Crucifixion," had been his lying reply. That meant being spread-eagled on the wheel of a gun limber, tied to the spokes at wrist and ankle, with the toes off the ground and the entire weight of the body on the outraged nerves and muscles of those members.

Lacking a gun limber, the Germans used a post with a crossbar for this man's case. After that, this was a recognized mode of punishment for many petty offences in this camp.

It is true that this form of punishment is a part of the so-called discipline of our army. But it was not meted out for offences of the nature of this man's and if it had been, the obvious thing for the sergeant-major to have done would have been to have lied like a man; instead of which he piled horror on horror for his own countrymen. I have the facts and names of these cases.

There will be many strange tales to come from these camps in the fullness of time. No doubt some will go against us, but the truth must be told at all costs, else the evil goes on and on.

We were sent out one day to dig potato trenches on the moors in a terrible rain. We stuck our spades in the ground and refused. The guards had French rifles of the vintage of 1870 which carried cartridges with bullets that were really slugs of lead. They began to load. A little *unteroffizier* tugged excitedly at his holster for the revolver.

A big Canadian stepped up: "Wait a minute, mate." He reached down to the little man's waist and drew the gun.

He offered it to its owner, butt forward, "Now go ahead and shoot, and we'll chop your damned heads off."

The rest of us confirmed our leader's statement by gathering around threateningly and making gruesome and suggestive motions with our spades. There were two hundred of us and only forty guards. We meant business and they knew it. They took us back to the *laager* and locked us up.

The following night, that of January 22nd, our guards were reinforced by thirty more.

Chapter 14

Four Miles to Freedom

Simmons and Brumley, together with my companion of the first escape, had determined to make a break for it with me. And although we were not quite ready at this time the addition to the guards forced our decision. We had a scanty supply of biscuits saved up and I had wheedled a file from a friendly Russian; Simmons got a bit of a map from a Frenchman; and we secured a watch from a Belgian. With this international outfit we were ready, except that we lacked a sufficient store of food. However, there was no help for that.

The *laager* was a twelve-foot-high barbed wire enclosure, eighty feet wide by three hundred long, with the hut occupying the greater part of the central space. There was sufficient room below the bottom wire to permit the trained camp dogs to get in and out at us.

They patrolled the four-foot lane that enclosed the *laager* and wandered up and down it, their tongues out, always on the alert. They were as well confined as we were, since the outer wall of wire was built down close to the ground. They were very savage and seemed instinctively to regard us as enemies; as all good German dogs should.

The sworn evidence of prisoners exchanged since my escape mentions that in one case an imbecile Belgian was daily led out to the fields, wrapped up in several layers of clothes and then set upon by the dogs under the guidance of their guards; this was for the better instruction of the dogs.

At each corner of the *laager* there hung an arc light. The

sphere of light from those at the end did not quite meet and so left a small shadow in the centre of the end fence.

As soon as night came we arranged that six other men should walk to and fro from the end of the hut to the shadow at the wire, as though for exercise. Others, ourselves included, clustered round the end of the hut. I watched my chance, and when the moment seemed favourable, fell into step beside the promenaders.

We swung boldly out, intent apparently, on nothing. Our arrival at the inner wire synchronized with that of one of the guards beyond the outer wire. We turned about without appearing to have seen him. Still walking briskly, we reached the hut and turned again. The guard's back was now turned; he was walking away. At his present rate of travel he should be twenty yards off when we next reached the wire. We dared not chance suspicion by slackening our gait. My heart stopped.

As we reached the shadow I fell prone and lay motionless. No dogs were in sight. Niagara pounded in at my ears but no hostile sound indicated that I had been observed. I dragged myself carefully through and under the clearance left for the dogs, until my cap brushed the lower wires of the main and outer fence. My feet still projected beyond the inner wire into the main enclosure so that on their next trip one of my comrades inadvertently touched my foot, startling me.

I held the strand in my left hand and fell to filing with my right so that at the snap there should be no noisy rebound of the spring-like wire. A post was at my right, and, the wire having been nailed to it, I was safe from this danger on that side.

The sound of the tramp of those faithful feet receded but the sound of them came strongly back to me like a message of hope.

By the time they were back once more I had cut through three strands and was crawling cautiously toward my objective, a pile of peat two hundred yards distant, which seemed to offer cover as a breathing spot and starting point. On the signal from the promenaders that I was through the wire, Simmons followed, and after him, Brumley. The other man lived up to the example he had previously set himself. He drew back in alarm and refused to make the attempt.

Thursday 6
1916

Jan 22nd Escaped from Vehnan-moor lager in company with Tom Bromley 3rd Toronto reg. Murven Simmons 7th B.C. reg. captured on the 27th

Friday 7

at the town of Latham on the river Ems six kilometers from Holland spent two days in civil jail at Meppen got little or very little food one days rations

Saturday 8

2 oz. bread 1/4 pint coffee 1 pint gruel

returned to Vehnan-moor on the 30th Jan after being marched through

RECORD OF SECOND ESCAPE AND RECAPTURE

With twenty-five guards all about and some only thirty feet away, the very impudence of the plan offered our only hope of success. I still lacked fifty yards of the peat heap when I heard three shots, next the dogs, and then the general outcry which followed the detection of Brumley.

I rose to my feet and ran. We had already mapped out our course in advance by daylight, for just such a contingency; so I struck boldly out. I was still in the swamp to my knees, and under those conditions even the short start we had might prove sufficient, since our pursuers would also bog down. The swamp was intersected by a series of small ditches and scattered bushes, which added to the difficulty of the passage. I heard Brumley floundering and swearing behind and went back to pull him out of a bottomless ditch. Simmons joined us while I was still struggling with him. In another hour Brumley's legs played out. We could still make out the lights of the *laager*. It was vitally necessary to push on; so we encouraged him as best we could and managed, somehow, to reach the edge of the swamp by daylight. We put ourselves on the meagre rations our store allowed, one biscuit for breakfast and another for supper, with a bit of chocolate on the side. We had apparently outdistanced the pursuit. We prayed that our friends might not be too severely punished for their part in our escape.

We lay in the heather all day, soaked to the skin with the brackish water of the swamp, the odour of which still hung to our clothes. It was January and very cold and sleep was impossible under such conditions. We nibbled our tiny rations and struck out as soon as darkness came. Our plan was to go straight across country, but Brumley could not navigate the rough going of the fields; although on the level roads he made out fairly well. So we chanced it on the latter.

Brumley was struggling along manfully but his legs caused him great suffering. At about two o'clock in the morning we lay to in the shadow of a clump of trees at the roadside, thinking to ease him a bit. He flung himself down. Simmons massaged Brumley's legs whilst I watched.

We had just said: "Come on," and they were rising to their

feet, when another figure stepped off the road and in amongst our trees. It was so dark where we stood that he probably would not have seen us had not Brumley at that very moment been rising to his feet. He appeared as much surprised as we were and started back as though in amazement. And then without more ado, he turned and fled the way we had come whilst we made what haste we could in the opposite direction, all equally alarmed.

Who he was or what he wanted, we could only surmise. If he was not also an escaped prisoner then he must have been badly wanted by the authorities to have been travelling in such a fashion at such an hour; and above all, to have been so alarmed by this chance meeting with fugitives. In any event we wished him luck and promptly forgot all about him.

Later on in the night our road led us directly into a village. We hesitated as to what we should do. Brumley was for pushing through. The alternative was to go round and through the fields, lose valuable time and play out Brumley's precious legs. It was past midnight, so we decided on the village route, and started on.

We passed through without being molested, but just as we were leaving the other side some civilians saw us and shouted "Halt!" and other words meaning "to shoot." We paid no attention. Espying a wood in the distance, we struck out for it. Brumley was in misery and threw up the sponge. We stopped to argue with him, at the same time dragging him along, and while doing so saw two more civilians rushing up and shouting as they came. Lights began to spring up all over the village. Brumley stopped dead and refused to go farther. We had previously agreed that if anything should happen to any one of us the others were to push on, every man for himself. No good could be gained by fighting when we were so hopelessly outnumbered, so Simmons and I rushed into the wood, swung around and out again and lay down on the edge of it, in time to see them take Brumley and come sweeping by us in hot pursuit. The main body stopped only a moment to inspect their capture, gathering around poor Brumley so that we could not at first see what had happened to him. Then several of them started back toward the village, with him limping along at their side. Ten yards away a knot of them gathered and assisted another up into a tree to watch for us. One handed him a rifle and the pursuit went on into the wood. Occasionally we heard the sentinel stirring.

We scarcely breathed. It seemed impossible that he could not hear the pounding of our hearts. We grew quite stiff in our cramped positions, but feared to shift a limb and waited for three-quarters of an hour before we dared to worm our way cautiously in the other direction. The snap of a twig was like that of a rifle on the stillness of the night.

Once we stopped, thinking that certainly he had heard us. It was only the beat of a night bird's wings. We dared take only an inch at a time, sliding forward on our bellies and then—waiting.

We met another sentry farther up, but worked around him in safety and with more of ease, as we were by this time on our feet.

Arriving at the end of the small wood, we walked boldly across the intervening fields to another one, large enough to afford cover for an army corps, and there felt comparatively safe.

We were, however, very wet and cold and altogether miserable, buoyed up only by the liberty ahead. As it was only two o'clock, we pushed on for several hours before stopping to lie by for the day.

For days we carried on thus without discovery. Each night was a repetition of the preceding one, an interminable fighting of our way through dark forests, into and out of sloppy ditches, over fields and through thorny hedges, dodging the lights of villages.

We went solely by the stars, which Simmons understood after a fashion, and, aided by our map, we held fairly well to our general direction. We had no other sources of information than our own good sense. We watched the sky ahead at night for the glow which might indicate to us the size of the community ahead; and aided by a close observation of railroads, telegraph wires and the quality of the wagon roads and the quantity of travel on them, were able to form fairly accurate estimates of where we were and which places to avoid. Except on unfrequented byways we travelled by the fields, hugging the road from a distance. This made travel arduous but safer.

At that, we were sometimes spoken to in neighbourly greeting. We grunted indifferently in reply, as an unsociable man might. When, as sometimes happened, people rose up in front of us from gateways or hidden roads, it was very disconcerting. On such occasions only the darkness saved us, for we took no chances, wherever there were lights.

It was really harder in the day time; when, try as we might, we could not count on avoiding for our hiding place the scene of some labourer's toil or perhaps the covert of some child's play. We slept by turns with one always on guard. It was difficult indeed for the guard not to neglect his duty, so utterly weary were we. The lying position we needs must retain all day long aided that tendency, and yet we were always so wet and cold that real sleep was difficult to secure.

In this district the swamps were numerous and difficult to cross. The small ditches and canals that drained them or the almost equally swampy fields added to our grief. The feet slipped back at each muddy step: We fell into ditches: Dogs barked: And we almost wept.

Once a dog helped us by his barking. It was night and we were crossing a very bad swamp, an old peat bog which was full of the ditches and holes that the peat had been taken from. These were full of black water which merged so naturally into the prevailing darkness that we repeatedly fell into them. We floundered out of one only to fall into another, uncertain where we were going and lost to all sense of direction. There was no vestige of track or road. It was then that the dog barked. We stopped to listen, conversing in low tones. Certainly, we thought, the dog must be near a house and that meant dry land and a footing. So we advanced in the direction of the sound, stopping to listen to each fresh outburst so as to make certain that we should not approach too closely. Apparently he had smelt us on the wind.

Before we reached the dog we felt the solid ground under foot and were off once more at a tangent from the sound of his barking.

The swamps were a great trouble to us, as were also some of the fields, so cut up by ditches and hedges were they, and yet, in order to avoid the roads and the wires, we frequently had to lay a circuitous route to avoid these obstacles or else chance the road, which we would not do. Often, when we could see our course lying straight ahead on the road, we put about and tacked off and away from it because a parallel course was impossible on account of the swampy nature of the ground. With these bad places passed we could perhaps pull back to our true course again, but only after double the travel that should have been necessary.

However, we did not mind that so much. Nor did we greatly mind the short rations we were on. The other privations were too severe for us to notice these minor ones.

The worst was the continual state of wetness and the resultant coldness of our bodies. It was not so bad at night when we were walking and so kept our blood circulating, but by day it was very bad. We used to pray for night and the end of our enforced rest. We were never dry or warm but were always very cold and miserable. The sun, on those rare occasions when it came forth, did not appear until ten or eleven in the morning. By mid-afternoon it was again a thing of the past. At best it was very weak and we had to hide in the bushes where it could not reach us. All we could do was to take off one garment at a time and thrust it cautiously out near the edge of our hiding-place to some spot on which the sun shone. Under these conditions we grew steadily weaker on our allowance of two biscuits a day; for the time of year precluded the possibility of there being any crops for us to fall back upon for food, and it was too risky a proceeding to attempt to steal from the householders.

On the eighth day we reached the River Ems. We had no difficulty in recognising it, as it was the only large one on our map that lay on the route we had chosen, and we had passed nothing even faintly resembling it, with the exception of some large canals, which were easily recognizable as such and which we had swum. We made out trees which appeared to be on the other shore.

We regretfully decided that it was too late to attempt the crossing that night. The daylight proved the line of trees to be merely the tops of a flooded woodland. The shore was a good

German prisoners marching

High explosives bursting over German trenches—British dead in foreground

quarter of a mile away. It was January; the water was cold and full of floating ice, and very swift. Fording was out of the question. For two days and nights we wandered up and down the bank, vainly seeking a boat or raft with which to make the crossing. We finally discovered a large bridge, which was submerged except for its flood-time arches. There was no sign of life and it looked safe, so we proceeded to cross. We discovered, however, that we had not reached the bridge proper, but were merely on the approach to it. We dropped off onto the main steel portion. The wind beat the cold rain against us so that we could neither see nor hear. However, we went on and were nearly across when suddenly a light flashed on us and we heard a startled "Halt!"

We could barely make out the mass of buildings that indicated the line of the shore. It seemed too bad to throw up the sponge so easily.

I said under my breath to Simmons: "We'll push right on," and loudly: "Hollander!" thinking we might perhaps get far enough away to make a run for it. But there was no show: It was too far to the shore.

There was a shouted command and the clatter of rifle-bolts striking home. It was no use. We stopped and shouted that we would not run, and then waited while they advanced toward us.

The elderly *Landsturmers* guarding the bridge gathered us in and took us over to their guardroom at the hotel. We judged the incident to be an epoch in the monotony of their soldierly duties. They were very good to us. Two of them moved away from the fire to make room for our wet misery and they gave us a pot of boiling water, two bivouac cocoa tablets and a loaf of black bread. The news spread, and civilians dropped in to stare at and question us. In the morning the entire population came to see the *Engländer* prisoners. We learned that we were only four miles from Holland, and cursed aloud. The town was Lathen and when, the next morning, we discovered that it was gaily bedecked with flags and bunting we decided that we were indeed personages of note if we could cause such a celebration. However, it was only the Kaiser's birthday.

In the afternoon they took us by rail to Meppen and shoved

us in the civilian jail, where we were allowed a daily ration of two ounces of black bread, one pint of gruel and three-quarters of a pint of coffee for two days, until, on January thirtieth, an escort came from Vehnmoor. They roped us together with a clothes-line, arm to arm, and marched us through the principal streets by a roundabout route to the station so that all might see.

We were unwashed, unshaven and so altogether disreputable as to satisfy the most violent hatred—such for instance as we found here. It did not require our pride to keep our hearts up or to keep us from feeling the humiliation of so cruel an ordeal. We simply did not experience the painful sensations that such a proceeding would ordinarily arouse in the breast of any man; just as after heavy shell-fire no man feels either fear or courage; he is too dazed and stupid for either. Many spat at us and good old *Engländer Schwein* came to us from every side. It seemed like meeting an old friend, after our few days away from it. The faces of these people were different from those we had left at camp but their hearts were the same. They lined the streets and jeered at us. But we were too tired and hungry to care.

And that ended that trip to Holland.

CHAPTER 15

In Napoleon's Footsteps

Upon arrival at camp, we were put in cells for eleven days while awaiting our court-martial.

During that period we suffered terribly from sheer starvation. The daily rations consisted of a poor soup and a small quantity of black bread. Hungry though I was, there was only one way by which I could eat it—hold my breath and swallow. I am aware that the Germans consider this food quite palatable but that may be because they are accustomed to it. It was to us the resort of starving men. The cells were quite dark—four-by-eight-foot wooden boxes. The confinement and short rations on top of our arduous journey, during which we had had nothing but the two biscuits a day, caused us to grow weaker daily.

Our friends, however, contrived occasionally to get portions of their food to us. They maintained a sentry of their own, whose duty it was to watch for and report our trips to the latrine. It was unsafe for us to ask for this permission more than once a day with the same guard. As the latter was frequently changed, however, we were enabled to work the scheme to the limit.

At the worst, this let us out of our cells for a few minutes; and, if we were lucky, enabled us to get a handful of broken food. Seeing us come out, the prisoner on watch would stroll into the hut and pass the word. Shortly, another would come out to us and in passing frequently manage to slip us something. On one long-to-be-remembered occasion, a man of the King's Own Yorkshire Light Infantry, managed to "square" the guard, a pleasant-faced young German, in some manner we could never fathom, so that the latter actually brought to us two spoons and a wash basin full of boiled barley, which we ate in the latrine. That was the most humane act experienced from German hands during my fifteen months' sojourn in Germany.

On the eleventh day we were marched out to what would be the Germans' orderly room. A Canadian who had picked up a smattering of German acted as interpreter. He did what he could for us, which was little enough.

Asked why we had tried to escape, we feared to tell the truth, that we had been forced to it by ill-treatment; so merely stated that we were tired of Germany and wanted to go home. The presiding officer said: "Well, you fellows have been a lot of trouble to us. I've been told to tell you that if you give us any more; we'll have a little shooting bee." We were sentenced to thirty days' dark cells. That was our court-martial.

One lucky thing happened to us here: When they took our map away it fell in two, as a result of having been folded in our pockets. The officer crumpled one piece up, made a handful of it and tossed it away, at the same time shoving the other half at me, which I eagerly clutched. That piece showed the portion of Germany adjoining the Holland border.

Our thirty days' dark cells were spent in the military prison at Oldenburg. As before, they were four-by-eight feet in size, but with a high ceiling which gave me room to stand on my hands for exercise. Each of us was confined alone. The walls and floor of the cells were of stone; the shutters, of steel which were always closed. There was no furniture other than the three boards which served as the mockery of a bed and which were chained up to the wall every morning. A small shelf which held the water pitcher was the only other furnishing. No ray of light was permitted to enter the place. The month was February but there were no blankets, and the place was unheated. The rations consisted of half a pound of black bread and a pitcher of water, which were thrust in to us every morning, so that except for the guard who unchained the boards at night we had no visitation in the twenty-four long, long hours.

I cannot remember that I brooded much. Rather, I let my

mind run out as a tired sleeper might, which was no doubt fortunate for me. My family were greatly in my thoughts. I wondered how my wife was making out and if she was receiving her separation allowance all right, for I had heard of many cases where the reverse had happened; and whether the boys were well and going to school. I hoped that all was well with them and that they did not worry too much over my lot.

As I was not permitted either to send or receive letters during the period of my trial and incarceration, my wife was in fact in great distress of mind about me as she received no word for many weeks and imagined the worst. And when at last I could write it was only to say that although I had been well I had been unable to write, leaving her to draw her own conclusions.

The cell door opened promptly at five o'clock every morning. We were allowed ten minutes in which to clean our cell, go to the lavatory and wash up, all under guard. These were the only occasions during which we had an opportunity of seeing one another or the other prisoners. These rites were all performed in silence, and communication of any description was forbidden and so keenly watched for as to be impossible. However, Simmons and I got what small comfort we could out of seeing one another frequently, and by this time there had grown up between us such a mutual respect as to make us value this highly. The other prisoners included Germans as well as our allies and there were some civilian German prisoners. The German soldier prisoners were mostly in for committing the various crimes of soldiering which in the British Army would have put them under the general head of defaulters. That classification, however, had been done away with in the German Army. The slightest infringement of discipline was punished with cells. Non-commissioned officers received the same punishment as the men, without, however, losing their rank, as would have been the case in our army.

Upon finishing the ten minutes allotted to us we were forced to re-enter our cells and stand against the wall, at the back, so that we could neither see nor communicate with one another until the guard got around a few minutes later and looked in to see that all was as it should be before slamming the door.

There was no use in trying to stretch the ration out for two meals. I tried to and gave it up. And after that I ate the bread, filled up on water and sat down on the cold stone floor for another twenty-four hours of waiting.

My thoughts dwelt greatly on food. We were supposed to receive soup every fourth day, but we did not. The prisoners of other nationalities did, and in addition were exercised regularly. At least we could hear the rattle of their spoons against their bowls and the tramp of their feet. The slow starving was, to my mind, the worst. And after that the loss of sleep. If one did drop off, the cold soon caused a miserable awakening. I tried not to think, and did all the gymnastic drill I knew, even to standing on my hands in the darkness of the cell. I knew that if I gave up it would be all off, for I could daily feel myself getting wobbly as the confinement and starvation, added to my already enfeebled and starved condition when I entered, began to tell on me. It must be borne in mind that I had already served eleven days' solitary confinement on insufficient food, after several days of jail on ditto, and eight days while escaping, during which I had been continually wet and without food, other than the two biscuits daily, before beginning to serve this sentence. Simmons, of course, was in the same plight.

The last day, that of February 22nd, rolled around finally. We were taken from our cells at nine o'clock and marched out for an unknown destination which we knew only as a stronger punishment camp than the others we had been in. Ahead of us we saw poor Brumley; but were unable to communicate with him, and I do not know whether he saw us or not. That was all we ever learned directly of his fate. His wife, in Toronto, has since informed me that he is still in Germany and has only lately been recaptured after another attempt at escape.

At eleven that night we arrived at our destination. This was the strong punishment camp of Parniewinkel, in Hanover, on the road over which Napoleon had marched to his doom at Moscow. We wondered if we, too, were going to ours.

We had had no food that day, nor did we get any that night, but were shoved into a hut full of Russians, who did not know what to make of us. We were so long of hair and beard, so ragged, so emaciated and so altogether filthy that they must have thought us anything but British soldiers.

Later we found that there were, in all, between four and five hundred Russian, eighty French and Belgian, and, including ourselves, eleven British prisoners, of whom Simmons and I were the only Canadians, all shoved into two huts in the middle of the usual barbed-wire *laager*.

As Giessen was the best camp, so this one was the worst of all those we were to know. It was not so wet as the swamp at Vehnmoor, but the drinking water was even worse than the brackish, peat-laden water there. The general sanitary arrangements were terrible and the food was worse than at Giessen, the camp in which that lack had been the worst feature among many bad ones. And on top of it all the treatment was very bad, much worse than any we had previously known.

A soup, made from a handful of pickled fish roe and a few potatoes, was a stock dish, and terrible to taste. On one night a week we received a raw herring fresh from the brine barrel, which we were supposed to eat raw and uncleaned, but could not. On one day in seven there was a weak cabbage soup and of course, a small daily ration of potato-and-rye bread. Fortunately, our parcels were beginning to arrive by this time, so that, in fact, we fared better than at any of the better camps, in the matter of food. With the Russians it was different, and we used to give our soup to them in exchange for their share of boiling water, which we used in conjunction with the contents of our parcels and which they had no use for anyway, especially for washing purposes.

It was difficult to get an opportunity to boil water for the making of tea or cocoa, even when parcels furnished the essentials, as there were so many men and so few stoves that it was a constant struggle to get near the latter.

However, as we had refused to work, we did not require very much food. We used also to give our black bread to the Russians, for which they insisted on doing our washing, though it was little enough of that they did for themselves. They were very good and simple men.

Ours was a good bunch of fellows and gave freely to one another and to the unfortunate Russians, who rarely received parcels. There was no selling or trading on misfortune here, as in some of the other camps we had been in. The Germans themselves were short of necessities here. They hated to come to the *Engländers* to buy, so used to send the Russians to beg for soap which they would not use in any event, and in this case simply sold to the guards. Discovering this, we shut down on indiscriminate giving. Soap or any other fatty substance was by that time very scarce in Germany, amongst the lower classes at least. I was the only "non-com" in our lot, and so put up the stripes I had taken down to avoid giving *Augen Rechts* at Vehnmoor. I used that authority now to persuade my fellow Britishers to give to the unfortunate Russians rather than to the French, who, like ourselves, were receiving parcels.

A boy of five years or thereabouts used to come regularly to the wire, upon which he would climb and hang like some foul spider on its web. Grasping it in both small hands and kicking vainly at it and us, he would scream: *"Engländer Schwein,"* and I know not what other names, spitting venom like a little wildcat. This was not the riffraff of the camp. The boy was the son of the camp Commandant, and the apple of his father's eye and the thing was often done under that eye and amid the vicious applause of the young father and his terrible crew.

The Commandant was a young chap, a lieutenant. What he lacked in years he made up in hate. He was known as an England hater. We were poison to him. The latrine, a mere shallow pit, was just outside the door of our hut and the Commandant saw to it that the latrine fatigue was always wished off on to the British. We were made to bail it out daily with buckets, which we then carried to the surrounding fields, on which we spread the contents while the Commandant and guards laughed. The *unteroffizier* in immediate charge of us, if left alone would not make us do this. He was the last kind German I remember, and I have mentioned all whom I can recall as having performed the slightest act of kindness to us, even of the most negative quality. He used to say that it was a pity to treat us so; that such a job was good enough for the Russians, who were no soldiers, anyhow, and who smelled bad and would not wash; but for us who were soldiers it was a great shame.

The vermin were so bad here that we chanced further trouble by writing on post cards as though to friends in England, and complained. We knew that they would be intercepted and go to the Commandant. They did. We were marched to Cellelaager to go through the fumigating machine. We went into a large hut, stripped, tied our clothes in a bundle and shoved them into the large oven to bake for five hours while we sat round with nothing on but a smile. In the interval we were made to run the clippers closely over our heads and bodies. There were sores on some of the Russians as big as a hand, eaten deep into by the vermin and the bones threatened to break through the skin of some as we sat about naked, shivering. Uncleanly at best and denied soap here, the lower class of them neglected all the rules of cleanliness. Their "non-coms" were the reverse, being almost without exception men of some education and general attainments.

Upon our return to this camp we were told by a friendly Russian in the orderly room that the post cards were being held there as evidence against us. We begged him to give them to us. He did so, and we had barely finished destroying them when a German officer, accompanied by a file of men, entered and demanded them. We explained that they had been destroyed. He would not believe us. We pointed to the charred ashes. He searched our bodies, our beds and the scanty furnishing of the hut, naturally without avail. The Russian orderly was severely admonished and our fire was cut off as punishment.

The treatment at this camp was uniformly bad. The next morning the *Raus* blew at four-thirty instead of five, as was customary. While we were still engaged in dressing the guards rushed in, some with fixed bayonets, others with them gripped short, as with daggers. The leader wore a button, the insignia of non-commissioned rank. He gave a berserker roar of rage and charged furiously at an inoffensive Russian and stabbed the poor fellow in the neck; while his victim lay back in pleading terror, with outstretched arms. And then, still roaring, he slashed a Frenchman who was walking past, on the back of the head. Going down the hut, he espied Harckum, of the East Lancashire Regiment, tying his shoes. Without warning he plunged at him, and, striking, laid open the entire side of the man's face, splitting the ear so that it hung in two pieces. This was all quite in order because we were slow in dressing.

The Russians, with the exception of a lucky few who received some from a Russian society in England, got no parcels, and suffered accordingly. They were more amenable to discipline than we were, and perhaps because of their hunger used to go out daily to work on the moors from daylight until dark. They were a cheerful lot, considering everything, little given to thinking of their situation and not blessed by any great love of country nor perhaps the pleasantest recollections of it; and to that extent at least appeared to be comparatively satisfied, even under ill treatment. Ill fed as they were, they used frequently to fall out at their work from sheer exhaustion, which the Germans said was only laziness and malingering and for which they would be returned to a point near the *laager*, where we were, for their punishment. By the Commandant's orders this consisted of forcing them to run the gauntlet of two lines of soldiers who jabbed them with bayonets if they fell into a walk—until the victims could run no more and dropped in their tracks. The Germans would then roll their eyelids back for signs of shamming, and if any such indications were shown, they were jabbed again—and usually were, anyhow—until their failure to respond proved that they were really unconscious.

This happened with alarming frequency on a regular schedule, forenoon and afternoon, to all Russians who refused to work. On one occasion we saw six or eight of them laid out unconscious at one time in this manner. We wished to do something for them, but were refused permission, and one man who was thought to be a ring leader was selected to make an example of; he was awarded seven days' cells.

We had previously agreed that if we were awarded this punishment; we should refuse to run the gauntlet and should let them do their worst. There was no more heard of all this, but after that the Russians were punished on the other side of a belt of trees just outside the *laager*, where we could not see them, though their piteous cries could plainly be distinguished.

Three of the Russians broke away from this camp, and finding themselves near the stores, crawled in the window and stole a half of a pig. They were recaptured, and, after doing thirty days' cells, were forced to work out the price of the pig at the rate of thirty pfennigs—or six cents—a day, which ordinarily would have been credited to them for the buying of necessities. And pork came high in Germany.

There was one kind of pill for all ailments. That however, may have been only stupidity. At least the practice is not confined to the prison camps nor the army of Germany, as all British soldiers know. But even these were not for the British.

On another occasion a party of Russians arrived from another camp twelve miles away.

They said that some Englishmen there who had refused to work had been shot at until all were wounded in the legs.

We continued to receive our old friend, the *Continental Times*, here, and through it first learned of the Skager-Rack or Jutland battle, in which, the paper claimed, over thirty major British ships had been sunk, in addition to a larger number of smaller ones. The *Times* said it was a great victory for the Germans. The last we doubted and the first we knew to be untrue, since some of the ships they claimed to have sunk had been destroyed previous to our capture, nine months before. It was in the *Times*, too, that we first heard of Kitchener's end. We could not believe it, and for a month laughed at the guard's insistence on the story, until one day a post card arrived from England, saying: "K. of K. is gone." That was a terrible blow to us, for to the British soldier; Kitchener was the tangible expression of the might of his Empire.

Some of our party of eleven British had been prisoners since Mons and they were in a very bad way. The poor food, the lack of the fundamental necessities of the human frame, the terrible monotony of the continual barbed wire, the same faces round them, mostly unfriendly, all combined to have a most depressing effect, not only upon their bodies, but upon their minds. Many of them will never be of any use again. Compared to Ladysmith, when that place was besieged in the South African War, the latter, terrible though it was, was far and away better than this, even if we did live on horse meat at the last in Ladysmith.

There was a certain amount of vice here, induced by the life. A kilted Highlander was accused of having fathered a child in a German family, where he had been employed. We did not learn the facts of the case; but such, at least, was camp gossip and it served to detract materially from the habitual despondency of our lot.

CHAPTER 16

The Third Escape

Simmons and I had been planning on another escape ever since our recapture. So we kept on our good behaviour, while we saved up food for *Der Tag*. We had hitherto refused to work, as had the remaining Britishers, but in order to keep ourselves fit; we finally volunteered to carry the noon ration of soup out to the Russians who worked on the moor. Our job consisted of carrying an immense can of soup, swung high on a pole from our shoulders, out to the workers, under guard of course. Starting at eleven each day and, by permission of the guard, occasionally resting, we were usually back by one o'clock. Each day we saved a portion of our food. We wanted twenty days' rations each, estimating that it would take us that long to walk to Holland. We specialised on concentrated foods from our parcels—biscuits, tinned meats, and so on. We had our cache in a hole, dug under cover of night, under the flooring of the hut. It was unsafe to keep food on our bodies or near our beds, as the guards were in the habit of calling the *Raus* at all hours, and sometimes, several times during the night. It might be at twelve, two or four, although it was never alike on any two nights in succession, except that they always searched us. We could see no reason for this; other than to break our rest and perhaps our spirits, as at Giessen Camp. Certainly, no one would carry any forbidden thing on his person, under such surveillance, and they well knew we could hide anything we wished in other places; as we did.

Each Saturday morning, Simmons and I paraded for paint.

We stood, while a big Russian, with a brush and bucket, painted large red and green circles on our breasts, backs and knees. Thin stripes were also painted down the seams of our trousers and sleeves and around the stiff crowns of our caps. This was to mark us as dangerous characters. As such we received more of the unwelcome *Raus* attentions than the others and were the more wary in consequence.

We were busy opening our mail on one of those rare occasions, when Simmons gave a startled exclamation. I looked up and saw him gazing curiously at a small cheese which he turned slowly around in his hand. As I stepped to his side, a guard came in. He hastily shoved the cause of the strange behaviour into his pocket. When the guard had gone; he passed me a letter to read. It was from his brother in Canada. "I received your letter all right and am sending you a special brand of cheese," I read—and understood.

We waited on tiptoe until night, to open the cheese. It was one of the cream cheeses, so popular in Canada, no bigger than my closed hand. We gingerly unwrapped the tin foil and broke it open. To our great joy, in the hollow heart of it there was tucked away the tiny compass Simmons had written for from Vehnmoor just before our second escape. With it were four American quarters.

Not anticipating this good luck, we had exercised our ingenuity to construct a rude compass of our own out of a safety-razor blade and an eyelet from my boot. It was within fifteen to twenty degrees of the true north. In addition we had a safety lamp, which one of the guards had long been looking for under the impression that he had lost it.

We now had our twenty days' rations saved up and so took turns sitting up at night, awaiting our chance. We spent two months in this watchful waiting, watching the wire and the sentries. But no opportunity offered. We took turn about, one man on watch all night long, every night. He could not seem to watch but must lie in his place, observing all movement in the hut and listening carefully for any indicative noises outside. Occasionally, he might step outside and ostentatiously walk about as though sleepless, and, if spoken to, say that he was not well.

But always there were the shining eyes of the watching dogs, growling, if one came too near, and outside the stodgy sentries; and above all, much light.

So we determined to volunteer for work, figuring that they were so short of men that they would not lightly refuse us. It so happened that ten men were asked for that Saturday to hoe turnips on a near-by farm. The pay was thirty pfennigs—or six cents—a day. We volunteered and were accepted without cavil. They thought our spirit gone and that we had accepted the inevitable. We reasoned that if we worked hard while we studied the lie of the land we might be asked for again, could go prepared, and make a break for it.

And so it fell out. We worked hard all that day, at the same time impressing the topography of the country upon our minds. At the close of the day we were taken to the farm for our supper of potatoes and buttermilk and then marched off to the *laager*, four miles distant. On the following Monday we were ordered to go out to the same place. Unfortunately we could not take our store of food as its bulk would have meant our detection. In addition to the equipment already mentioned I carried two packages of tobacco, a shaving brush and a box of matches. Simmons had a terrible razor which would not shave, four boxes of matches and a small piece of soap. These were all our worldly possessions. It will be seen that, true to our British tradition, the shaving outfit constituted the most formidable part of our impedimenta.

We worked all day. And so did the rain. We knocked off for supper at eight o'clock. The three guards escorted us to the farmhouse, but after locking the front door, went into an adjoining room with the farmer for their own meal. The back door was forgotten. We were famished, so fell to on the supper of buttermilk and potatoes. I finished first and strolled lazily over to the door. Besides Simmons, there were seven Frenchmen and an Englishman, all of whom were still at table and none of them aware of our plans. I carelessly opened the door and stood on the sill a moment. Still pouring. "Come here, Simmons, and see this. We're going to get wet before we get back." Simmons shoved his chair back and joined me. We both stepped outside and gently shut the door.

Once more we were on our way! We found ourselves at the edge of the village in which the farmers hereabouts had their homes. We worked our way carefully round the outskirts and made for a bit of a wood a mile and a half away. We were only half way to our objective when the village bells began to ring. Once more the hue and cry was on!

When the deep baying of the dogs joined in we said "Ataboy!" cast aside all concealment and began to run for it. We reached the wood safely enough, but it turned out to be only a thin fringe of trees, offering no concealment whatever. We dashed through them. On the other side a village opened up. Back to the wedge of wood we went. A good-sized ditch with a foot or so of water in it ran along the edge of the wood. Its sides were covered with heather, which drooped far down into the water. We flung ourselves into it, after first shoving the tin box containing our precious matches into the heather above. Pitch darkness would not come until ten o'clock. During the intervening two hours we lay on our backs in the water with only the smallest possible portion of our faces projecting. Once the guard jumped over the ditch less than four yards away. We suffered intensely, for, although it was late August, the water was very cold.

When things had become quiet and daylight had passed we withdrew ourselves from the muck, and after rubbing our numbed bodies to restore the circulation, struck out across the country, intent on shoving as much distance as possible between ourselves and the camp before another day rolled round. We knew that the alarm would be out and the whole country roused, with every man's hand against us. We were getting used to that. I, for one, had determined not to be taken alive this time. But I certainly did not want to be put to the test. So we ploughed our way through oat and rye fields and over and through ditches—many of them. Once we stripped our soggy clothes off to swim a river that faced us. In no place did the water come above our knees; but what it lacked in depth, it made up for in coldness. We saw none of the humour in that, so we cursed it and stumbled on, two very tired men. We pulled handfuls of oats and chewed dryly on them as we plunged up to our waists through the crops.

We reckoned that we had made thirty miles by morning and apparently had outdistanced our pursuers.

One night early in our pilgrimage, we espied some cows in a field. Simmons had been a farmer in Canada and so was our agricultural and stock authority here. He plunged through the hedge to see if he could not capture a hat full of milk whilst I stood guard outside. I stepped into the shadow of some trees, and occasionally I could hear a guarded "Soo—Cow!" footsteps—and then as like as not, a muffled curse. I smiled.

Two figures came hurriedly down the road. I pressed back against the hole of the tree, holding my breath. It was fairly light on the road and to my amazement I saw two men who wore French uniforms. Also they had heavy packs on their back. That last meant but one thing—food.

I rose to my feet: *"Kamerad!"*

One of them stopped short. The other pressed on. He muttered something under his breath and the other broke into a trot to catch up.

I edged along, trying desperately to be friendly. That made them the more timid. They would have none of me. No further word was exchanged just then except for a repetition of my *"Kamerad."*

I whistled softly to Simmons. That alarmed them the more. They lengthened their stride. So did mine.

One said something I could not catch. They half halted and made a brave attempt to pose as Germans, to judge by their guttural talk and brassy front.

I could not explain, although I tried in the half light to show my friendliness, and Simmons, now a few rods away, did likewise. I endeavoured to address them in French—and could not. I tried German. That was worse and the final result—chaos.

All I could think of was *"Kamerad."* I kept on like a parrot, foolishly repeating it.

All this took but a moment and then they were gone and we after them.

So there were they, walking hurriedly, fearful of us for Germans no doubt and casting uneasy glances back. I followed slowly, at a loss to know what to do, my eyes glued on the inviting squareness of their heavy packs. Simmons jogged behind, endeavouring to catch up. The moon laughed at all four of us.

"Come on," I said. "They're Frenchmen. We'll follow them. They have two packs on their backs! Grub! And maybe we can bum them for a bit."

Simmons needed no second invitation but set out as eagerly as I in cautious pursuit; so fearful were we of alarming our quarry. Our eyes were glued on their packs.

Just then the road opened up into a broad expanse of heather. And there we lost them. We beat about in the heather for a long time, and called loudly, but without avail. They were no doubt lying down, hiding.

We found some potatoes in a field that night, dug them up with our bare hands and ate them raw. We were very sad when we thought of those packs.

It was, I remember, on the day following that we saw some of the lighter side of German life. The woods thereabouts were cut up into big blocks, as city streets are. We were laying to in one of them, thankful for the thickness of our shelter when we heard laughing voices and then a gust of laughter as a flying group of girls and boys romped past. They played about for half an hour, causing us great alarm by their youthful fondness for sudden excursions into unlikely spots, after nothing in particular. The oldest of the group, a sizable boy of seventeen or thereabouts and a pretty girl of near that age, hung back long after the younger children had passed on. We had little to fear from them. They were quite evidently engrossed in one another. He argued earnestly, while she listened with a half-smile. Once, he made as if to take her hand but she drew back and stiffened. He ignored the rebuff. A moment afterward he said something that pleased her so well that the last we saw of them his arm was about her waist as they went down the path together.

Parniewinkel lay forty to fifty miles northeast of Bremen, which in turn was one hundred and fifty miles from the Holland border. We reckoned on having to walk double that in covering the stretch, and figured on twenty-one days for the trip.

May   Sunday 21   1916

Aug 21st Escaped with
Mervin Simmons 8-30 P.M.
lay 2½ hrs in ditch very
heavy rain storm made about
18 Kilometers very heavy going

Aug 22nd Still raining soaked

Monday 22

and cold found good
cover breakfast dinner &
supper Turnips & Oats we
have a good supply Tobacco
15 Kilometers

Aug 23rd Rain stopped &
milder fair cover
but still soaked confident

(1st horman escape)

Tuesday 23

meals for the day Peas &
Oats very heavy going
swamps

SALIENT DETAILS OF THE THIRD ESCAPE

My diary for that day, August 22, 1916, reads: "Still raining. Soaked and cold. Breakfast, dinner and supper: turnips and oats." The night was a repetition of the preceding one, and made worse by the number of small swamps we had to struggle through. The next day's diary reads:

> Rain stopped and not so cold. Fair cover; still soaked but confident.

We had our first narrow escape that day. We were lying in the corner of a hedge. It was so misty as to give almost the effect of night, but so long past day as to make travelling unduly dangerous. When the mist lifted we found ourselves within fifty yards of a thickly populated village with just a narrow strip of field between. We could hear all the early morning bustle of any village, the world over. This was about three o'clock. An old man followed by a dog made straight for us. I had just come off the watch, which we took turn about. Simmons whistled cautiously to me, the very sound a warning to be quiet.

I looked up. The old man wandered along the hedge and stood over him for several minutes.

It was very trying but he lay motionless, for fear of the dog. A blow would have sufficed for the old man. The latter remained so for a couple of minutes, standing over him, busy.

The meals for that day were peas and oats. It was a slow way of making a meal. We liked the oats the best and pulled some whenever we came to them, if our pockets were not already full, so that they should always be so. We ate them as we went, from the cupped hand, spilling some and spitting out the husks of the others which sometimes stuck in our throats, making them very raw.

For August twenty-fourth the diary reads:

> Very hard night. Crossed about five kilometres of swamps and numerous canals. Bad accident. Clothes went to the bottom, but recovered. We are soaked, as usual, and only made about eleven kilometres. Are outside town of Bremen. Cover very poor. Meals for the day: Nix. Still confident.

The cover ranked before the food as an item of interest to us. Knowing the general direction of Bremen from the camp, and that it was much the largest town in the vicinity, we experienced no difficulty in locating it by the reflection of its lights against the sky.

August 25th: More rain and cold. Hiding on the bank of the Weser. Better going last night. Going to look for boat tonight. River two hundred yards broad. Socks played out. Made pair out of a shirt. Met a cow. Meals for day: turnips, carrots and milk.

August 26th: More rain. Found boat and crossed river. Hedges grown so close and so many of them, we have to go around them. Takes a lot of time. Otherwise going good. Meals for the day: turnip, peas and oats. Met another cow. Frisked her. Cover none too good. Trying to dry our clothes in sun. More confident.

We always became more confident at the slightest semblance of warmth.

The socks we made out of a shirt which came from the clothes-line of some *haus-frau*. We made "Dutch" socks in Western fashion by cutting out large diamond shaped pieces of the cloth, which when the foot was placed on it, folded up nicely into a sock of a kind.

The cow, or rather, her milk, was the greatest treat of all.

It required some searching before we found a boat. We finally discovered a boat house which we broke into and by great good luck found inside it a boat which answered our purpose. Our chief concern was lest the owners might raise a hue and cry against the theft. However, when we reached the further shore we gave the boat a good push out into the stream so that if they attempted to follow our trail they might find the boat a long ways down stream.

August 27th: Rain left off. Trying to dry ourselves in sun. Had a hard night keeping clear of town. Good cover in a wood. Meals: turnips and another obliging cow. Feet pretty sore. No socks. Still in the best otherwise.

The town in question was the second one we passed after leaving Bremen. We saw the reflection of its lights in the sky and thought that we should easily miss it. But suddenly from some high ground we found ourselves working directly down on the streets so close below us that we could discern people going to and fro. We turned and fled.

Swinging well round to the south we thought at last to clear the town easily, instead of which we again came up against it, in the outskirts this time. And we repeated that disheartening performance a couple of times before we cleared the obstacle and once more swung on our way.

It was such occurrences as this that disheartened us more than anything else, even the great hardships. To labour and travail, to do the seemingly impossible, night after night and then in the snap of a finger to find all our pains, all our agony gone for nothing, reacted on us terribly at times.

On the following morning we met with our second narrow escape, under much the same circumstances as the first. We had crawled into a hedge toward the heel of the night, and rather earlier than usual on account of a thick mist which prevented us from holding to our course. When it lifted we made out the slope of a house roof shoving itself out of the grey fog directly in front of us. Our hedge divided two fields, in both of which labourers were already cutting the crops. In this hedge, on each side of us, were gateways so close together that when, as occasionally happened, people passed through one, we were forced to crawl up to the other to avoid detection. We had done so again when, without warning, a drover came plodding up behind his sheep. We had no time in which to go back up the hedge. The sheep crowded from the rear and overflowed at the narrow gateway into the hedge where we lay and so ran over our bodies. We remained quiet, thinking he would pass on; but what with the frightened actions of his sheep and the yelping of the dog his attention was inevitably attracted to the spot where we lay. He came over, looked down at us, but said nothing and stalked on. We were uncertain as to whether he had seen us or not. Numerous incidents of a similar nature had made us overconfident. We had previously escaped detection in some very tight corners by simply lying quiet. Casual travellers had all but walked on us upon several occasions, and at night we ourselves passed many people and thought nothing of it.

A moment later the shepherd walked off directly toward the labourers, glancing back over his shoulder at us as he did so. We struck out at once, before the crowd could gather. We had, at the beginning of this, our third escape, agreed not to be taken alive to go through a repetition of the torture of mind and body which we had already undergone, and, perhaps for this time, worse. And it was understood that if one played out the other should carry on. Each of us had a stout club and could have made a tidy fight.

Concealment was useless and, furthermore, impossible. We passed close by a group of the harvesters and headed for a wood that lay on the other side of them. They could not mistake either the vermilion circles on our khaki tunics, faded though they were, nor our wild and dilapidated appearance, which was not made more reassuring by the clubs we carried. Glancing back, we saw them gathering hurriedly in little knots.

We reached the wood, flung ourselves down and watched them until dark, during which time they made no attempt to follow us. Nor did we see any sign of other pursuers, though we kept on the *qui vive* all night, as we trudged through the interminable fields, forcing our way through tight hedges and plunging waist deep into the water of small canals.

CHAPTER 17

The Fight in the Wood

The only roads we habitually used were side ones, and especially did we avoid any with telegraph wires which might be used against us. It was a flat and swampy country, full of mist, and the nights were few in which it did not rain. And we were always very wet and very cold. The latter was worse than the lack of food. Sometimes we struggled for hours at a time, knee-deep in desolate stretches of mist-covered morasses which gave no promise of firm footing but which often dropped us in to the waist instead. In addition, the country was cut up by numerous small ditches, six to eight feet wide, which along toward morning presented so much of an effort in the jumping that we usually plunged into the water by preference. Our feet were adding to our misery by this time. On one occasion, as we dragged ourselves out of the water, two dogs came rushing at us and then followed, yelping. It was nearly daylight and a woman came down to see what was going on. We remained motionless near a hedge. She failed to see us, which was perhaps good luck for both her and us.

The diary for that period reads:

August 28th: Rain worse than ever. Not a piece of our clothes dry and too much water to lie down. Good going last night. Cover in a wood outside village. Good. Meals: Nix. Ought to reach the Hustre river tonight. In good spirits.

August 29th: Rain stopped and a bit of sun came out. Feeling much more cheerful. Just had a shave and clean-up.

Going last night very bad. Swamps and canals. Had to leave our course. Feet feeling better. Meals for the day: turnips, peas and green apples. Did not reach the river. All's well. No complaints.

That shave was a terrible torture.

August 30th: Rain, thunder and lightning most of last night. Got a bit of shelter in a cowshed in a field. We are wet and cold as usual, with no sun to dry. Fair cover in a small wood. Going good last night. Haven't struck the Hustre yet. Meals: green apples and brambles. Feet pretty sore. Made a needle out of wood and did a bit of sewing. Best of health.

We had been ploughing through the mist, confused by it and the numerous hedges, when at the side of a small field we had run into this cowshed, a tumbledown affair of sods, caved in at the sides and partly covered by a thatched roof. We built up the side from which the wind came the worst, hung a rotting canvas we found at the other end and then snuggled up together to exchange warmth.

The mist had scarcely lifted when we heard a slight noise. We looked up. A woman was at the entrance to our hovel, looking down full at us. She turned and walked away. We rose, still dazed with sleep, and found that we were quite close to a farmhouse which owing to the mist we had failed to observe before, and from which our visitor had evidently observed the result of our building operations. "She saw us," I said, and we regretted not having seized her. She appeared to be signalling.

A good-sized wood lay well up ahead. "Come on," I said. "Let's beat it. We can handle a few of 'em better than the whole mob."

We could see the farm labourers gathering in a knot. The rain came on just then and perhaps assisted in dampening their ardour. At any rate they did not follow us into the wood. We spent rather an uneasy time though, when, late that day, some men approached our hiding place in a clump of bushes and for half an hour shot their fowling pieces off all around where we lay.

They did not seem to be after us; more likely they were hunters. The same thing had happened in a lesser degree several times before. None the less it was very uncomfortable to have the buckshot rattling all around us in the bushes where we lay and we felt much better when they had gone.

As for the wooden needle: That was of course the result of our necessity. It was a long thorn—first, a punch in the cloth and like as not a stab in the finger in the bargain, then a withdrawal of the crude needle and a careful threading of the hole with our coarse string, after the fashion of a clumsy shoemaker. Some sewing! Some needlewoman!

The green apples and the berries which we got here proved a most welcome change in our diet.

August 31st: Not much rain but very cold. Too dark to travel last night. No stars out to go by. Crossed the river this morning, at last. Good cover in bushes. Feet are badly peeled. Hope for better luck tonight. Meals: apples and turnips. Cold and rain are putting us in bad state. But still confident.

We were daily growing weaker and prayed only that our strength would last to put us over the border.

September 1st: No rain and a little sun. Feeling much better. Going last night much the best we have had. Good cover in a thicket. Will soon be going over the same country we did last time we escaped. Meals: peas and beans. Still in good health.

September 2nd: No rain, but cold out of the sun. Pretty fair going last night. Feet still sore. Cover on straw stack in middle of field. Warmer than the woods. Zeppelin just passed overhead going north. Meals: turnips, carrots, apples and peas.

September 3rd: Fine weather. Good going last night. Feet still pretty bad. Had to cut my boots. Fine cover in the wood. Meals: baked potatoes. Feel fuller.

This was our first cooked meal and the pleasure it gave us was beyond all words. We lit it under cover of night so that by the time day had come there was nothing but glowing coals in which the potatoes roasted while we slept.

My feet were badly swollen by this time so that I was faint with the pain of them.

The Zeppelin, strange though it was under the circumstances, was only a small incident in many others of vaster importance which were happening daily to us but it was flying so low that we deemed it best not to move until it had passed. We wondered if it were going to England, and envied it.

> *September 4th*: More rain. Hard going half the night. Crossed large peat bog and wet to the waist. Very cold. Cover in wood. None too good. Got scared out of our first cover. Meals: Milk, apples and peas. Feet not so sore. Still raining and cold. We should soon be at the River Ems.

On the evening of this day we walked out to the edge of the wood we were in and stood there sizing up the near-by village. It was about seven o'clock and wanted about an hour to darkness and our usual time for hitting the trail. Without any warning, a burly farmer confronted us. He was as badly startled as we were. Our remnants of painted uniforms and our ragged, soaked and generally filthy condition no doubt added to our terrible appearance. We had long since lost our caps and our hair was matted like a dog's. The German was armed with a double-barrelled shotgun, and at his heels a powerful-looking dog showed his teeth to us, so that I marked the red of his tongue. If he raised the alarm we were done for. We still had our cudgels.

I do not know whose was the offensive. But I do know that the three of us came together with one accord in a wild and terrible medley of oaths in two languages and of murderous blows that beat like flails at the threshing. Simmons and I struggled for the gun which he tried so hard to turn on us, the dog meanwhile sinking its teeth deep in our unprotected legs and leaping vainly at our throats; while we felt with clutching fingers for his master's, intent only that he should not shout.

In those mad moments there sped through our brains the reel of that whole horrid film of fifteen months' torture of mind and body; the pale, blood-covered faces of our murdered comrades of the regiment, the cries of the patient Russians behind the trees, and our own slow and deadly starvation and planned mistreatment. All these, and God only knows what else, should be ours again if we should be recaptured.

We were near to Holland. In fancy and by contrast we saw the fair English fields and the rolling beauty that is Ontario's; we heard the good English tongue and beheld the dear faces of our own folk. We bore that farmer no ill will. And his dog was to the last a very faithful animal, as our clothes and limbs bore true witness. We had no ropes. And we were two very desperate men, badly put upon.

We dropped his gun in the bushes, together with the body of his dog; and passed on. It had not been fired and we had no desire to have the charge of carrying firearms added to the others against us if, in spite of all, we should be so unfortunate as to be recaptured.

CHAPTER 18

Safe Across the Border

September 5th: Stopped raining and a little warmer. Got our clothes dry once more. Cover in a wood outside a small town. Going last night good, after we had crossed another peat bog. Meals: milk, baked potatoes and apples. Hope to reach the river tonight. Bad feet. Best of health otherwise.

September 6th: No rain and warmer. Heavy dew. Fairly good going. Best of cover. Had a fire. Pretty comfortable. Milk, potatoes, apples.

September 7th: Still fine weather. Very poor cover in a hedge. Good road to go on. Made pretty good time last night. Feet feeling better. Running out of tobacco. Otherwise in the best and still hope the same. Meals: potatoes and beets.

We spent a great deal of time discussing ways and means of adding to our stock of tobacco. Any smoker knows what it is to want the weed. Consider then our half famished, wet and utterly weary condition. It was a real necessity to us. We discussed waiting at the roadside until a man with a pipe appeared; when we should rob him. We dismissed that as too hazardous. It would be necessary to kill him and that seemed a bit thick for a pipe of tobacco. So we did the only thing that was left to do—cut down our already scanty rations of tobacco and took scrupulous care to smoke to a clean ash every vestige of each heel of old pipe, but in spite of that our supply became exhausted.

September 8th: Lovely weather today. Good going last night in small swamp. Good cover in a forest on the banks of the Ems. We will try to cross tonight. Meals: potatoes and mangels. Our final try for liberty. Feel good for it.

We had arrived at the river at two o'clock that morning, too played out to attempt the crossing then. We retraced our steps to a potato field, dug some of the tubers and, when daylight came, lit a fire and roasted them. We were in a dense forest of young trees, so that by lighting the fire before the mist lifted, the latter hid our smoke. We remained unperceived, though we could hear voices and footsteps on every side.

September 9th: Swam the river and two canals. Crossed a large swamp. No rain but very cold. Think we are over the border. Very poor cover in a hedge. Wet to the skin. Clothes got soaked but in best of spirits and confident.

We went down to survey the river shortly before dusk and found it both broad and swift. We went back again and tore a gate from its hinges, carried it the five hundred yards down to the river and then stripped for the crossing. The gate was not big enough to carry us but answered for our clothes. Simmons swam ahead, guiding it, while I shoved from behind. We made the crossing without mishap but straightway fell into one of the worst experiences of the entire trip. We plunged into a swamp which took us five hours to get through. There were moments when we all but gave up and thought we should never get out. At times we sank in it up to our waists, particularly after leaping at the numerous tufts of grass which seemed to promise a footing that they never realised and which sometimes sent us in it to the armpits, so that we were sure we were doomed to be sucked down for good in the filthy mess.

The fearful odour that our plunging around stirred up, naturally aided our nervous imaginings and it was undoubtedly the worst trial we had yet met with on the journey. I cannot convey the black despair which took possession of our hearts at the seeming hopelessness of all our efforts to find firm footing or a break in the landscape which might indicate a change in the nature of the country, a light, a voice, anything that would help to lift from our hearts the feeling of utter isolation from all human assistance and the seeming certainty that a few bubbles would be the only indication that we had struggled there. The darkness of the night intensified these thoughts. The rain did not matter. In fact it helped; for we were covered with the worse than water of the morass.

We looked at one another. We dared not speak. Anyhow, to do so was not our custom at such times as these. But each knew. A dull anger took possession of us at the thought of so inglorious an end after all that we had suffered to attain our freedom. With a prayer in our hearts we cast ourselves forward and somehow, sometime, found at last that we were safe and so flung ourselves down in our stinking clothes to lie like dogs in a drunken stupor that reckoned not of time or of our enemies.

We discovered an apple orchard here, in which the fruit was ripe. All the apples we had had up to date had been of the small and green variety. And even they, with the occasional milk, represented our all of luxury, so that these seemed indeed the food of the gods. We proceeded to fill up and after eating all that we thought we could, filled our pockets until they bulged, and started off, each carrying an armful of the fruit. At every step we dropped some. We stopped again and ate our surplus to make room. We refused to lose any of them. We came to a river, stripped, tied our clothes up in a bundle and proceeded to swim across, shoving the clothes ahead. I lost control of mine and they sank. I dived repeatedly in the darkness before I found them. The cargo of apples in the pockets made a bad matter worse. I should rather have drowned than have lost my apples. The possible loss of the clothes worried us very little. We had already decided in that event to waylay some German Michel rather than to go naked into Holland. However, by alternately dragging the bundle behind and swimming on our backs with it held high on the chest with one hand, we made the crossing, apples and all.

We were sitting in the shadow preparing to dress and wondering whether we were really over the border and if we could safely walk abroad, when we heard men walking toward us. We knew them to be Germans by the clank of the hobnailed boots which all our guards had worn. We had not a stitch on and our hearts were in our mouths. The patrol of six men stopped within five yards of us and then passed on within five feet and did not see us. We dressed quickly and went on, only to find a canal, for which we had to strip again.

Arriving at the other side; we dressed in the shadow of the bank, crawled to the top and plunged through the heather on to a road which we had almost crossed, when there came a cry of "Halt!" The patrol must have been standing in the trees where we had broken out from the heather, and very quietly, too, for we had lain for five minutes to make certain that all was safe. Evidently we were on or near the border if the number of patrols was any indication. We were not certain whether these were Hollanders or Germans. We made one big buck jump. "Fire, Gridley, when ready!" I left the entire knee of one trouser leg on a clutching thorn. But the patrol did not fire.

And then another canal. "I'm fed up with swimming tonight."

"So am I," agreed Simmons. "There are houses over there. There must be a bridge."

We slunk along the bank and to our joy found a small bridge. We dashed across it and debouched safely into a tiny village. Here we saw a difference, especially in the houses and the roadway. It was in the very atmosphere, a result no doubt of instincts made keen by the hunted lives we had led. On either side the fields stretched out, criss-crossed by a perfect network of small canals and ditches, which also served as fences.

We knew we were in Holland.

We deemed it unwise to show ourselves as yet, distrusting the sympathies of the Hollanders and fearful that they might give us up; and continued this policy until the next day. However, we took a chance and stuck to the road, a treat, indeed, to feel a firm footing after our weeks of travelling across country fields. This enabled us to shove thirty miles between us and Germany by morning.

It was not quite daylight when we espied a cow in a field at the roadside and gave chase. There was no other food in sight,

Private Merwin C. Simmons of the 7th Battalion, 1st Division, Canadian Expeditionary Force

so when our quarry threw up its tail and bounced off; we set out grimly to run our breakfast down. It was half an hour later that we corralled it in a corner between two broad ditches and were already licking our chops in anticipation; when we discovered that our cow was only a big heifer. Twenty-four hours earlier it would have been a tragedy. As it was, we only laughed. Such is liberty.

At this distance from the border we felt that we were safe from the Germans but were very much afraid that we might be interned. So we holed up in a farmhouse which had been partly burned down and built a roaring fire out of the remains of the charred furniture, placed some of the potatoes that were lying about in the fire, made a rough bed and went to sleep. Awakening later in the day, we raked the blackened potatoes out of the ashes and filled up on them. We were a fearful team; absolutely filthy, uncombed, unwashed, unshaven, and with the Russian's paint still thick upon us. Afterward we went down to the canal and endeavoured to knock the worst of it off. All danger was past now. We seemed to walk on air. We were once again British soldiers. And so fell to abuse of one another, finding fault and grousing; as all good British soldiers do when they are well off. I made out to shave Simmons. The terrible razor had never been sharp and lately had rusted from its travels. Simmons swore lustily and threatened me, ordering me at the same time and in no uncertain terms; to desist from the torture.

"Well, we want to go into Holland lookin' respectable. What'll they think of British soldiers if they see us? Have a heart!" I expostulated.

"Don't give a damn! I've had enough for being a Canadian; but I won't stand for this." I left him with his beard still on in patches and the bare spots bleeding angrily. As I had already committed myself, I had to bear in silence his purposely clumsy handling of that hack-saw. It was terrible, and Simmons, the scoundrel, laughed like a demon.

CHAPTER 19

Holland at Last

The diary summarizes the later events of that day:

September 10th: Fine weather and in Holland. All our troubles are over. We struck a small town called Alboom where the people did everything they could for us. Plenty of food. Slept in a house!

A man smoking a big pipe and wearing baggy breeches and wooden shoes came up and surveyed us with kindly amusement, as Simmons scraped at me with infinite gusto. He was a Hollander; not a "Dutchman." We soon learned that the latter was a term of contempt applied by the former to the Germans.

I asked him for some tobacco, which he readily gave to us from a capacious pouch. He waved his pipe at us in friendly fashion and said something which we took to be a question as to our identity. "English," we said, and in desperation turned to our scanty stock of French: "*Soldats; prisoniers.*"

"*Engelsch!*" He boomed. We nodded. He simply threw his arms round first one and then the other, so that I wiped the ashes from his pipe out of my eyes. He lumbered off and shortly returned with a counterpart of himself. He talked rapidly to his companion and waved his pipe. We made out the words "*Duitsch,*" "*Engelsch,*" and enough of others to know that he was telling our tale as he imagined it.

Our fears coming uppermost, we gave voice to them: "Intern?"

"No intern. *Engelsch.*" The other took up the cry: "*Engelsch goot! Frient.*" However our suspicions would not down.

The first man pointed out to the canal where a barge lay and made us understand that it was his. He wanted us to work our passage on it down the canal with him. They invited us by signs to go on board the barge for breakfast, an invitation which we joyfully accepted. We rowed out to the barge and sat down in the tiny cabin. The meal was plain. On the centre of the table was a loaf of brown bread, quite good enough it was true, but so reminiscent of the perennial black ration of the Germans that my gorge rose at the sight. Out of the corner of my eye I saw a white loaf on the shelf, the first in fifteen months. I caught Simmons eyeing it. We exchanged guilty looks but were ashamed to ask for it. They offered us the brown loaf and delicious coffee. I thought perhaps that if we exhausted the brown loaf the other might be forthcoming. I kicked Simmons on the shins and fell to on it, and, as opportunity offered, thrust pieces in the pockets of my tunic until, to our relief, they brought out the white bread, which we devoured to the last crumb. It was very good.

We filled our pipes in high contentment and went ashore, where a procession of enthusiastic villagers waited to escort us to the village. Men, women and children, wooden shoes and all, there were four hundred of them. The men all shook hands and pressed money on us. The women cried and one white-haired old lady kissed us both. The quaint little roly-poly children ran at our sides, a half dozen of them struggling to hold our fingers in their chubby fists.

The procession started off, the burgomaster leading, the two sailors and ourselves coming next. Some one behind dragged out a mouth organ and struck up *Tipperary*, and men, women and children all joined in. It was glorious. We sang, too, in English, and they in their tongue. The result was so ridiculous a medley that I smiled myself; but it made no difference. The spirit was there; we were happy.

Arriving at the village the *burgomaster* took us to his home and sat us down to a steaming breakfast, while a few of the chosen were invited in to watch us polish it off. The crowd remained outside, choking the road. Some of the bolder of the children crept slyly in the door, others peered shyly at us from the crack of it. And one little chap, braver than his comrades, clumped sturdily up to my knee, where he stood clutching it in round-eyed wonder and saying never a word for the rest of the meal, envied of his mates.

Not until we had leaned back, not contented, but ashamed to ask for more, did our hosts give vent to the curiosity that was eating into their vitals. An interpreter was found and they led us out to the road so that all might hear. The crowd flocked around while the officials questioned us. Many were the smothered interjections that went up from the men and exclamations of pity from the women as our tale unfolded. And the warm sympathy of their honest faces warmed our hearts like a good fire.

We started off on our triumphal course again. We were repeatedly invited into houses for something to eat. We accepted seven such breakfast invitations during the next two and a half hours and stopped only out of shame. We were still hungry. Every one gave us cigars, immense things, which projected from every pocket and which we carried in bundles under our arms. There was no refusing them. They were the insignia of the entente. And the coffee! The good, honest, Holland coffee with no acorns in it! I doubt if our starving bodies could have carried us many days more on the uncooked roots we had been living on. The motherly housewives, in their Grecian-like helmets of metal and glass that fit closely over their smoothed hair like skull-caps, bustled merrily about, intent only on replenishing our plates and cups, full of a tearful sympathy which was as welcome as their food.

Later in the day the officials took us to the police station at———. We became very much alarmed again. They read our thoughts and a subdued murmur of: "No intern, no intern," swelled up. The local burgomaster came to us. His first words, and in good English, too, were: "Have something to eat." We did. And then more cigars. The police were a splendid lot of men. They loaded us down with gifts and asked perfunctory questions for their records. One of them, H. Letema, of———, took us to his home, where his comely wife and daughter loaded the table with good things; while he brought out more cigars. He showed us to a bed-room before we understood where he was taking us. We refused, for reasons of a purely personal nature. "Nix," we said, and when he would not accept our refusal we tried it in *Niederländer*. "No, no." Still he persisted, and his good wife too. So we led him firmly aside and showed him the indescribably verminous condition we were in. That convinced him. They appreciated that little touch and gave us a deep pile of blankets, flung down on three feet of sweet-smelling straw in an outhouse, where we slept as we had not slept for many months.

In the morning Letema escorted us down to Aaschen, which was the nearest large town. A Belgian and a Holland lady, hearing of the escaped English prisoners, met us within twenty minutes of our arrival, took us in hand and loaded us down with kindnesses. We ate only five full sized meals that day, not counting the extras we absorbed between them. And there were more cigars. The raw oats and potatoes seemed a long way off.

Our day at Aaschen was a repetition of the previous one at Alboom and Borger, but on a grander scale. The ladies took us down to Rotterdam and did not leave us until they had turned us over to the British consul there, whose name I have forgotten but who, with the vice consul, Mr. Mueller, was very kind indeed; in fact, all whom we met, irrespective of their nationality, age or sex placed us under eternal obligations to them. In particular Mr. Neilson, the rector of the English church and in charge of the Sailors' Institute there, seemed to live only for us.

Mr. Henken at the American consulate was equally kind. They lodged us at the Seaman's Rest, took our painted rags away and clothed us in blue "civvie" suits which seemed to us the height of sinful luxury. We were shaved, clean and could eat everything in sight, at any time of the day or night. And did so. The meals we used to shift! We were very glad to get rid of our waterproof suits—for that is what they had become, from the paint.

Mr. Neilson took us sight seeing every day. Once we went out to Mr. Carnegie's Peace Palace which had been closed on account of the war but which we were permitted to inspect. I had not thought such buildings were done, except in dreams. It made our own bitter past seem unreal. The Italian room, in particular, seemed like a delicate canvas in marble and done in a fashion the memory of which gripped me for days and still haunts me. We spent days thus; supremely happy.

We were joined here by Jerry Burke of the 8th Battalion of Winnipeg. He was a nephew of Sir Sam Hughes, the then Canadian Minister of Militia and had just made his escape from some other camp. We were to have left on the fifth with a fleet of boats which sailed then. By the time we had got on board, however, the sailors from the first boat were returning. They had been torpedoed. And that stopped us. We got away on the S.S. *Grenadier* on the sixteenth, and after hugging the length of the English Coast, arrived safely at Newcastle-upon-Tyne on the eighteenth.

Here our troubles began!

CHAPTER 20

It's a Way They Have in the Army

My family in Canada have since remarked that although my letters had invariably been cheerful throughout my imprisonment, from the time I set foot on English soil they reflected the deepest despondency. That could be explained in part by the fact that uncheerful letters could not pass the German but could pass the British censor. But more particularly it was due to the fact that I became entangled in the interminable red tape of the army system, and, instead of meeting with the warm sympathy that an exile longs for, met, on the part of the army, with cold suspicion; however kind some individuals were to me.

Simmons and I were not permitted to leave the boat until the military came for us. So far so good. We were taken to the headquarters of the General Officer Commanding that district. He briefly examined us and good-naturedly gave us some money out of his own pocket and tickets to London, where we were ordered to report at the War Office.

Arriving in "The Smoke," as the army has named that city, we proceeded the next morning to 14 Downing Street and sent our names in to the official we had been directed to by the general. He was in mufti, whoever he was, and received us kindly enough. We were closely questioned about our experiences, particularly in relation to our guards, food, treatment, and so on. He also asked us as to the amount of sickness among the prisoners, the condition of the country, and so on.

Dismissed, we made a dash down past Big Ben and the Parliament Buildings for the Canadian Pay and Record Office,

The cemetery at Celle *Laager* Z 1 Camp

Corporal Edwards (second from left) after his escape. The two gold bars on his left coat sleeve indicate that he has been twice wounded

where at Millbank it overlooked the Thames. A sergeant took our names and after a time took us, too, in to the paymaster. Simmons drew his money without difficulty but I found that I was fifteen months dead and was told that I could get no money until my identity was re-established. I protested; so much so in fact that I fully expected to land in the "clink." No use. I was sent out on the street talking to myself.

We next called on Lady Rivers-Bulkeley and Lady Drummond to thank them for the very great kindness of themselves and the Canadian Red Cross in sending us our parcels regularly, and without which we would assuredly have been too weak to have made our escape. Lady Farquhar, the wife of our late commanding officer, was out of town, so we did not see her, much as we desired to thank her for similar kindnesses.

Simmons was single. He was sent to Canada at once and was promptly discharged. I had a wife and family awaiting me there and I wanted badly to go to them by the next boat. My wife had been receiving letters from me during my fifteen months' imprisonment; she had regularly received her separation allowance; the Canadian Red Cross and many kind friends in London had been sending me prisoner-of-war parcels for a year; the authorities admitted my identity and my former comrades recognised me; I had fifteen months' pay at $1.20 a day, besides a subsistence allowance of sixty-five cents a day, coming to me; but could not draw a cent of it. I was dead. And continued so for three months. There is no explanation. "It's a way they have in the Army"; or so the army says.

In the end it was only through the active intervention of Sir George Perley, the Canadian High Commissioner in London that my case was righted. He, I believe, cabled the Ottawa authorities, who in turn got in touch with my wife, who produced the necessary documentary evidence to prove that I had been alive and a prisoner all this time.

I went to the depot at Seaford. I borrowed from my old friends. I hung round the pay office. The paymaster said I was not on the strength of the regiment. I was old soldier enough to profit by that calamity at least. The bitter injustice of such miscarriage of justice blinded me, as I think it eventually does most soldiers, to the accepted code of civil life. I refused to attend roll call or do drills, fatigues, or any other part of my regimental duties other than certain interesting and thrice-daily rites not unconnected with the kitchen.

It is the commonness, the constant repetition of such stupidity and such lack of action that so much injures the reputation for intelligence of the army in the minds of those who have served in it; so that those who know it best, like it least—and put up with it only because it is the poor instrument of a good cause.

The paymaster fell sick. A young subaltern was acting for him. My sergeant pal tipped me off. As I have said, I was an old soldier with all that that implies. He marched me up to the officer, already more or less at sea about his new duties. I asked for money. He was aware of my history but not of the tangle I was in:

"How much?"

I wondered how much the traffic would bear.

"Twenty quid, sir," I ventured. He went up in the air.

"Impossible! I'll give you ten."

I O. K'd that while the words were yet warm on his lips. Fifty dollars is a great deal of money to a soldier. He gave it to me with a pass for Scotland—where I had relatives—to which I had long been entitled but which had been useless to me as long as I had no money.

I quickly gathered my cronies together and we packed into the canteen to celebrate the occasion fittingly, in the only fashion a good soldier knows, in army beer so thick and strong that the hops floated on the tops of the mess-tins. While searching for the bottom of one of these I heard the orderly shouting: "Corporal Edwards! Corporal Edwards!" The other men gathered round me in the corner, drinking, while I scrunched down so that the orderly passed on and out still shouting my name.

I fled to the tent and was hastily getting my things together when a corporal came hot-foot saying that the officer wanted me at once. I went in, gave him my very best regimental salute and stood at attention.

"I find that you are not on the strength, corporal, and are not entitled to any money, so I'll trouble you to return that money I gave you."

"I'm sorry, sir," I said sadly, "but it's gone."

"Gone? How?"

"Debts, sir," I said firmly. "My mates have been keeping me going."

"Well, you must get it back from them at once and return it to me. It's most irregular. Push on now and see that you're back here in an hour's time with that money before those fellows spend it all in the canteen."

"Very good, sir." I gave him a smashing good *Augen Rechts* to cheer him up against the time he should discover that I was well on my way to Scotland.

And I remained there until I received notice that my regimental bones had been officially exhumed; after which I had no difficulty in getting my back pay and three months' furlough for Canada and home!

Author's Note

An amusing and at the same time gratifying sequel to this story developed immediately upon the heels of its publication in a considerably smaller form in the *Saturday Evening Post*. Sergeant Edwards, who had not previously been consulted by the authorities, was at once offered his choice between doing "duty" in Canada or taking a discharge from the army, instead of going overseas again. He chose the discharge.

An interesting fact in connection with Brumley, the man who was the first to be recaptured on the second attempt to escape, is that according to a post card received from him by his wife, he has since made two other unsuccessful attempts at escape. Scarfe, who was exchanged to Switzerland, reports that he has married a Swiss girl there. Stamper, another Patricia who was captured at the same time as Edwards, has recently been exchanged and is now in England. Scott, who was captured with the men of an English regiment, was exchanged to Switzerland and recently returned to Toronto and has been in hospital, in a serious condition, ever since. The fate of the others is unknown.

The Evidence in the Case

In order to remove any vestige of doubt in the reader's mind as to the authenticity of Corporal Edwards' tale, it has been deemed advisable to present reproductions of certain newspaper articles and correspondence which bear directly on some of the points touched upon in the story.

It will be noticed that quite aside from the major fact of the escape itself having been brought out here, there is the equally important one of the bringing out of a great number of lesser points which tally to a hair with such references to them as are made in the story, such for instance as the references to the delay in England, the references in their post cards of those fellow-prisoners who remain in Germany and other facts of a similar nature.

The following are exact reproductions in every case, except for the explanatory note which prefaces each item.

EXTRACT FROM TORONTO DAILY STAR, MAY 30, 1915

Was Back Only Three Weeks
Corp. Edwards, Reported Missing
Was Wounded Short Time Ago

Lance-Corp. Edward Edwards of the Princess Pats who is reported missing today, has only been back at the trenches for three weeks, after having been wounded and in England for a month with a bullet in his foot. He lived at 70 Standish Avenue, Rosedale, where his wife and three young sons now live. He is 38 years of age and has been in Canada ten years. Previous service in Africa and India with the Gordon Highlanders is to his credit.

LETTER FROM CORPORAL EDWARDS TO HIS WIFE IN TORONTO

E. Edwards
Giessen (Allemagne)
Oct. 2nd, 1915

My Dearest Em: A few more lines, hoping they find all in the best of health and everything going on all right. I received your parcels all right. They were a treat and came in good condition. How are the boys getting along? Awfully sorry about Hector but hope he is all right again, poor chap's been having a hard time of it. How are Gordon and Frank. Tell them I was asking for them. I guess the Beastie has grown quite a big chap. Thanks for J. Birnies' address. I will drop him a card some time but you see I can only send two letters a month. Jack wanted me to write to the lodge but I can't see how I can manage it. Em, lass, don't send me any clothing as I will manage all right. Col. Farquhar's wife is going to send me out some and Major Gault is sending tobacco and cigarettes so I will be all right. I had a parcel from Bob with a shirt and some eatables; also one from Jean at Blacktop and one from home. We are always on the lookout for them. Have you had any word from Mina? I've had letters from them all.

We are having rather cool weather. I sent a post card to G. Nelson; I don't know if he ever got it but you can ask him when he comes up. Em, what are you doing about the house? Are you getting it fixed up or are you coming over home? It would be rather late this year to come over but please yourself; only let me know what you are doing. Is George still in Canada? Jean was expecting him to drop in any time. He has been very good to me ever since I landed first in England. I will never be able to pay her back. I can't

give you any news as I don't know it myself. Don't wait on a letter from me before you write but write often and tell me all about yourself and the boys. Tell Jack to write and I will drop him a card when I can. Keep your heart up and look after yourself. Tell Miss Holmes I was asking for her; also Mrs. Arlow. Tell her I got her letter; also tell all my friends I was asking for them. If Mr. Skerrow comes up again tell him I am doing fine but would sooner be working up in N. Toronto—but am making the best of it. I think I will stop Em; I have really nothing to tell you, only write soon and often. Give the boys a tight one for me. Best love to you all. Good bye.
Your Affect.
Ed
149 Corpl. E. Edwards
Barrack A.
Company 6
Prisoner of War
Giessen
Germany

P.S. Just received your letter Sept. 3rd. Tell Mrs. Bownie not to bother sending anything. I have got all I want. Can't send a long letter. This is all we are allowed. *Ed*

EXTRACT FROM MONTREAL GAZETTE, SEPT. 21, 1916

Edward Edwards Escapes From Foe
Toronto Soldier With Two Others Make Get-Away
Wander For Three Weeks
Brass Band Escorts Them to
Mayor of Town In Holland

London, Sept. 21.—Registered as dead by the Canadian Pay and Record office, which was about to authorise distribution of their effects, Lance-Corp. Edward Edwards of the Princess Patricias, 70 Standish Avenue; Pte. James Jerry Burke (1216) Eighth Battalion, Winnipeg and Pte. M.C.

Simmons (23445) of Seventh Battalion, Port Arthur, have arrived in London after having escaped from a German prison camp. They experienced some strenuous adventures. For three weeks they were at large; slowly and cautiously wending their way to the Holland frontier, they covered the distance of 150 miles. In Holland the fugitives to their surprise, found a warm welcome. In fact, a local band headed them in procession to the Mayor, who in turn communicated with the British Consul, with the result that they were shipped to England.

EXTRACT FROM TORONTO DAILY STAR, SEPT. 22, 1916

Mrs. Edwards is Rejoicing
Can Hardly Believe That Husband Escaped From German Prison
Heard So Many Different Tales
Comrades Who Have Returned Assured Her He Would Get Away

"I cannot believe it until I hear from him. But I do hope it is true. I am glad I never kept him back, and never told him not to go. He is a soldier to the backbone."

Mrs. Edward Edwards, 70 Standish Avenue, Rosedale, was discussing the report that her husband, Lance-Corp. Edward Edwards of the Princess Patricias, had escaped from a prison camp in Germany and after travelling over 150 miles of country arrived with two others on Dutch territory whence they were shipped to England after being fêted by some of the people in Holland.

"I have heard so many different stories. At first I was told he was killed, but later he sent me a letter from Germany telling me he was in a prison camp there. Only last Saturday I had a letter from him in which he asked me to send him on a box of soap to wash his clothes. He said in that letter that he had enough tobacco, cocoa and coffee to last him for some time but he needed soap."

Lance-Corporal Edwards, who was connected with the Royal Grenadiers, in Toronto, was formerly a member of the Gordon Highlanders, and fought with the 2nd Battalion of that regiment throughout the South African War. Stationed in India at the outbreak of that war the regiment was sent to South Africa and was shut up in Ladysmith. He is the possessor of three medals and five clasps. He took part in the great Delhi Durbar.

"Over a year ago my husband was shot in the foot," said Mrs. Edwards. "He returned to the trenches and was just three weeks back when he was posted as missing. That was a year ago last May. For a long time I had no word of what had happened to him until I had a letter from him."

Visits From Comrades

"Many of the returned Princess Patricias come to see me. Only last Sunday one of them said to me when talking of my husband:'He will be escaping from the Germans some of these days.' And it is just like him to do that. But he and the two with him must have suffered terribly in the time they were hiding through 150 miles of the enemy's country. I wish I had him home now."

"I heard from him regularly every six weeks by letter. Occasionally he would send me a postcard between the letters. He never discussed the war, except in the phrase that it could not last for ever. He always wrote bright and cheerful letters."

At No. 68 Standish Avenue lives the widow of Private Percy Edwards, brother of Lance-Corporal Edwards. Private Edwards was a reservist of the Gordon Highlanders and at the outbreak of the war was called home to join his regiment. He was killed in the first action in which the Gordons were engaged. His widow and three young sons live next door to Mrs. Edwards, who also has three young sons. Both of the Edwards brothers and their wives are natives of Aberdeenshire, Scotland.

Postal Cards to Mrs. E. Edwards
70 Standish Ave., N. Rosedale, Toronto, Ont., Canada

12th Sept. 1916
Assen
Holland

Dear Em: I guess you will get my letter along with this card explaining things. You will know that I have escaped from Germany and am on my way to England but will write you every chance I get. Give my love to the boys and I hope all is well at home. I am feeling pretty good. This is where I am just now. Yours ever, *Ed*

Sept. 8th
Newcastle-on-Tyne
England.

Dear Em: Hope you have received all my letters that I have written you from Holland. They will tell you all about my escape. I leave here for London tonight. Will write you from there. Love to the boys. Write me Bulter address. *Ed*

Sept. 22nd, 1916
Folkestone
England

Dear Em: Hope you got the cable all right, also some of the letters and cards I sent you. What do you think of my escape? Not so bad, eh? Write me at Bulter. How are the boys? Give them my love. Am back at Shorncliffe with the regiment. Will be going on leave. Trying to get over to see you. Will write you tomorrow. Write as soon as you can. *Ed*

Post Card to Cpl. E. Edwards
7 St. Mary's Place, Cuttor, Aberdeenshire, Scotland
from Cpl. E. Hardy, a fellow prisoner

Cpl. E. Hardy
Giessen (Allemagne)
25-9-1916

Dear Ted: I received your P.C. quite safe. I did a little dance

Homeward bound—Corporal Edwards in centre

on my own. Charlie Walker is away somewhere. How are Dennie and Nobler going on. You may be sure I was pleased to hear of you getting in port safe. Sorry to hear you got wrecked on your first trip but you have no worry now. Good Luck. *Ted*

POST CARD TO CPL. E. EDWARDS
NUMBER ONE COMPANY P. P. C. L. I., ST. MARTINS PLAINS
SHORNECLIFFE, ENGLAND, VIA HOLLAND
FROM HOOKIE WALKER, A FELLOW PRISONER

C. Walker
Giessen (Allemagne)
Oct. 1st, 1916
Dear Old Ted: I received your P.C. God Bless you and good Luck be with you always. I have been on the water and got wrecked also but I have not given up by any means. I am in the best of health. Remember me to all and God be with you. *Hookie*

UNDATED POST CARD TO MR. E. EDWARDS
ST. MARY'S PLACE, CUTTER, ABERDEENSHIRE, SCOTLAND
VIA HOLLAND, FROM CPL. HARDY

Cpl. E. Hardy
Giessen (Allemagne)
Dear Ted: I am very glad everything went on A1. I am sorry I was not with you. I am not wanting anything, thanks. I hope you have a good time when you go to Canada. I have not seen anything of Hookie for about 12 months, nor Stamper. I have still got a few things safe for you when I come home. I will close with best respects, *Ted*

UNDATED CARD TO MRS. EDWARDS

Rotterdam
Holland
Dear Em, Hope you are getting my letters all right and that

all is well at home. I am still feeling and getting treated pretty good and will be in England in two or three days. Since it all goes well write me c/o of Bulter address and I will be sure to get them. How are the boys? Is the wee chap still holding my place? Tell Gordon when I get to England I will help him get a bicycle so that he can be the same as Hector. This is where I am just now but will be on my way in a few hours. I have sent you Tinnie's photo. How will she do? It might be all we can get. *Ed*

Postal Card to Mrs. Edwards
70 Standish Ave., N. Rosedale, Toronto, Canada

Folkestone
26-10-16
Dear Em: Arrived back in Folkestone all right. Called on Mrs. Cawthra. Had a long talk with her. Can't get any word of when I am to get over to Canada but will let you know as soon as possible. Might be some time yet. Got the letter with Hector's and will bring the things with me when I come home. How are the boys getting along? Wish I was there. Goodbye. *Ed*

Extract from *Toronto Daily Star*, December, 1916

Home On Leave After Escape From the Huns
Sgt. Edward Edwards Tells Graphic Story of 100 Mile Flight
Wife Had to Prove Husband Was Alive
Sent His Photo and Letters Before War Office Would Believe It

No bands played and no Reception Committee extended the welcome hand to Sergt. Edward Edwards when he stepped off the train at the Union Station and walked to the home of his wife and family one day last week, after two years and seven months' absence at the front with a storehouse of thrilling experiences that rival even the exploits of the Three Musketeers. That he was one of only 49 left of the crack Princess Patricias who were mown down at the Ypres Salient on May 8, 1915, was wounded twice, missing and officially declared dead and escaped twice from German prison camps in company with two companions are only incidents in a long chapter of events which surpass in thrilling interest Dumas' most daring fiction. Tom Brumley, another member of a Toronto regiment, and Mervin Simmons, a Canadian from Trail, B.C., were the two friends of the modern D'Artagan, but unfortunately Brumley was recaptured by the Huns during the first escape and Sergt. Edwards has not heard from him since.

Sergt. Edwards is now on ten weeks' furlough and is due to report in England on May 10, when he expects to go into the fighting again. "We went to the Ypres salient in May. I was one of ten in my company to get through," said he.

Tribute To Col. Buller

Here Sergt. Edwards paid a tribute to his late commanding officer, Col. Buller, who was killed on the 2nd of June of this year. "It was the Germans, too, who told us of our old Colonel's death. They knew everything, it seemed, about our commanders and could tell the regiment and division that we belonged to."

We were taken to Roulers, Belgium. After a brief stay there we were taken to Giessen. There were 1,200 prisoners, mostly Russian and French. The food we got was awful.

Refused To Work

"After a stay here of about six months I was sent with my two friends, Brumley and Simmons, to a punishment camp for refusing to work in a steel factory to make munitions. Three hundred British and Canadians also refused in spite of threats, and ill-treatment, and all were sent on to Celle *Laager*, the main punishment camp. We were there two weeks and then we were split into small parties and I was slated with my two friends for a place called Oldenburg. Here they wanted us to go into a moor and drain the place to grow potatoes. It was from this place that we made our first serious attempt to escape.

"We made a dash for the shelter of the moor. In a few minutes we heard the baying of a vicious pack of dogs they had sent in pursuit, but we managed to elude them and struck out for the Dutch border more than 100 miles distant. We came to the River Ems four miles from the border of Holland. We could not find a boat or raft and were recaptured."

Made Final Escape

After undergoing this sentence, Sergt. Edwards and Simmons were taken to another punishment camp at Salsengen and it was from here that they made their successful escape on August 21.

The British Consul at Rotterdam arranged the wanderers' passage to England, where they arrived on the 18th of September. When he reported in London, Sergt. Edwards had to prove he was alive, because the records of the War Office had him marked up as dead. A lot of red tape had to be untangled before the gallant soldier could be officially brought back from the dead, but at that time he was still writing to his wife, so that, when she saw her husband's name in the casualty list, she at once contradicted the officials by sending her husband's letters and his pictures.

POSTAL CARD TO CPL. E. EDWARDS
SOUTH CAMP, SEAFORD, SUSSEX, ENGLAND
FROM CHARLES SCARFE, ALSO CAPTURED ON MAY 8TH

Manor Farm
Interlaken
Switzerland
Jan. 3rd, 1917

Dear Old Pal Teddy: Just a card hoping to find you well as it leaves me A-1. Hope you had a good Christmas. Had a fairly good one myself but hope we are in Canada next one. Have had enough of being a prisoner of war. Remember me to all the boys and write soon. From your old pal, *Charlie*

ALSO FROM LEONAUR
AVAILABLE IN SOFTCOVER OR HARDCOVER WITH DUST JACKET

DOING OUR 'BIT' *by Ian Hay*—Two Classic Accounts of the Men of Kitchener's 'New Army' During the Great War including *The First 100,000 & All In It.*

AN EYE IN THE STORM by *Arthur Ruhl*—An American War Correspondent's Experiences of the First World War from the Western Front to Gallipoli and Beyond.

STAND & FALL by *Joe Cassells*—A Soldier's Recollections of the 'Contemptible Little Army' and the Retreat from Mons to the Marne, 1914.

RIFLEMAN MACGILL'S WAR by *Patrick MacGill*—A Soldier of the London Irish During the Great War in Europe including *The Amateur Army, The Red Horizon & The Great Push.*

WITH THE GUNS by *C. A. Rose & Hugh Dalton*—Two First Hand Accounts of British Gunners at War in Europe During World War 1- Three Years in France with the Guns and With the British Guns in Italy.

EAGLES OVER THE TRENCHES by *James R. McConnell & William B. Perry*—Two First Hand Accounts of the American Escadrille at War in the Air During World War 1-Flying For France: With the American Escadrille at Verdun and Our Pilots in the Air.

THE BUSH WAR DOCTOR by *Robert V. Dolbey*—The Experiences of a British Army Doctor During the East African Campaign of the First World War.

THE 9TH—THE KING'S (LIVERPOOL REGIMENT) IN THE GREAT WAR 1914 - 1918 by *Enos H. G. Roberts*—Like many large cities, Liverpool raised a number of battalions in the Great War. Notable among them were the Pals, the Liverpool Irish and Scottish, but this book concerns the wartime history of the 9th Battalion – The Kings.

THE GAMBARDIER by *Mark Severn*—The experiences of a battery of Heavy artillery on the Western Front during the First World War.

FROM MESSINES TO THIRD YPRES by *Thomas Floyd*—A personal account of the First World War on the Western front by a 2/5th Lancashire Fusilier.

THE IRISH GUARDS IN THE GREAT WAR - VOLUME 1 by *Rudyard Kipling*—Edited and Compiled from Their Diaries and Papers Volume 1 The First Battalion.

THE IRISH GUARDS IN THE GREAT WAR - VOLUME 2 by *Rudyard Kipling*—Edited and Compiled from Their Diaries and Papers Volume 2 The Second Battalion.

AVAILABLE ONLINE AT
www.leonaur.com
AND OTHER GOOD BOOK STORES

ALSO FROM LEONAUR
AVAILABLE IN SOFTCOVER OR HARDCOVER WITH DUST JACKET

ARMOURED CARS IN EDEN by *K. Roosevelt*—An American President's son serving in Rolls Royce armoured cars with the British in Mesopatamia & with the American Artillery in France during the First World War.

CHASSEUR OF 1914 by *Marcel Dupont*—Experiences of the twilight of the French Light Cavalry by a young officer during the early battles of the great war in Europe.

TROOP HORSE & TRENCH by *R.A. Lloyd*—The experiences of a British Lifeguardsman of the household cavalry fighting on the western front during the First World War 1914-18.

THE LONG PATROL by *George Berrie*—A Novel of Light Horsemen from Gallipoli to the Palestine campaign of the First World War.

THE EAST AFRICAN MOUNTED RIFLES by *C.J. Wilson*—Experiences of the campaign in the East African bush during the First World War

THE FIGHTING CAMELIERS by *Frank Reid*—The exploits of the Imperial Camel Corps in the desert and Palestine campaigns of the First World War.

WITH THE IMPERIAL CAMEL CORPS IN THE GREAT WAR by *Geoffrey Inchbald*—The story of a serving officer with the British 2nd battalion against the Senussi and during the Palestine campaign.

STEEL CHARIOTS IN THE DESERT by *S.C. Rolls*—The first world war experiences of a Rolls Royce armoured car driver with the Duke of Westminster in Libya and in Arabia with T.E. Lawrence.

INFANTRY BRIGADE: 1914 by *Edward Gleichen*—The Diary of a Commander of the 15th Infantry Brigade, 5th Division, British Army, During the Retreat from Mons

HEARTS & DRAGONS by *Charles R. M. F. Crutwell*—The 4th Royal Berkshire Regiment in France and Italy During the Great War, 1914-1918.

TIGERS ALONG THE TIGRIS by *E. J. Thompson*—The Leicestershire Regiment in Mesopotamia During the First World War.

DESPATCH RIDER by *W. H. L. Watson*—The Experiences of a British Army Motorcycle Despatch Rider During the Opening Battles of the Great War in Europe.

AVAILABLE ONLINE AT
www.leonaur.com
AND OTHER GOOD BOOK STORES

ALSO FROM LEONAUR
AVAILABLE IN SOFTCOVER OR HARDCOVER WITH DUST JACKET

A JOURNAL OF THE SECOND SIKH WAR by *Daniel A. Sandford*—The Experiences of an Ensign of the 2nd Bengal European Regiment During the Campaign in the Punjab, India, 1848-49.

LAKE'S CAMPAIGNS IN INDIA by *Hugh Pearse*—The Second Anglo Maratha War, 1803-1807. Often neglected by historians and students alike, Lake's Indian campaign was fought against a resourceful and ruthless enemy-almost always superior in numbers to his own forces.

BRITAIN IN AFGHANISTAN 1: THE FIRST AFGHAN WAR 1839-42 by *Archibald Forbes*—Following over a century of the gradual assumption of sovereignty of the Indian Sub-Continent, the British Empire, in the form of the Honourable East India Company, supported by troops of the new Queen Victoria's army, found itself inevitably at the natural boundaries that surround Afghanistan. There it set in motion a series of disastrous events-the first of which was to march into the country at all.

BRITAIN IN AFGHANISTAN 2: THE SECOND AFGHAN WAR 1878-80 by *Archibald Forbes*—This the history of the Second Afghan War-another episode of British military history typified by savagery, massacre, siege and battles.

UP AMONG THE PANDIES by *Vivian Dering Majendie*—An outstanding account of the campaign for the fall of Lucknow. This is a vital book of war as fought by the British Army of the mid-nineteenth century, but in truth it is also an essential book of war that will enthral.

BLOW THE BUGLE, DRAW THE SWORD by *W. H. G. Kingston*—The Wars, Campaigns, Regiments and Soldiers of the British & Indian Armies During the Victorian Era, 1839-1898.

INDIAN MUTINY 150th ANNIVERSARY: A LEONAUR ORIGINAL

MUTINY: 1857 by *James Humphries*—It is now 150 years since the 'Indian Mutiny' burst like an engulfing flame on the British soldiers, their families and the civilians of the Empire in North East India. The Bengal Native army arose in violent rebellion, and the once peaceful countryside became a battleground as Native sepoys and elements of the Indian population massacred their British masters and defeated them in open battle. As the tide turned, a vengeful army of British and loyal Indian troops repressed the insurgency with a savagery that knew no mercy. It was a time of fear and slaughter. James Humphries has drawn together the voices of those dreadful days for this commemorative book.

AVAILABLE ONLINE AT
www.leonaur.com
AND OTHER GOOD BOOK STORES

ALSO FROM LEONAUR
AVAILABLE IN SOFTCOVER OR HARDCOVER WITH DUST JACKET

WAR BEYOND THE DRAGON PAGODA by *J. J. Snodgrass*—A Personal Narrative of the First Anglo-Burmese War 1824 - 1826.

ALL FOR A SHILLING A DAY by *Donald F. Featherstone*—The story of H.M. 16th, the Queen's Lancers During the first Sikh War 1845-1846.

AT THEM WITH THE BAYONET by *Donald F. Featherstone*—The first Anglo-Sikh War 1845-1846.

A LEONAUR ORIGINAL

THE HERO OF ALIWAL by *James Humphries*—The days when young Harry Smith wore the green jacket of the 95th-Wellington's famous riflemen-campaigning in Spain against Napoleon's French with his beautiful young bride Juana have long gone. Now, Sir Harry Smith is in his fifties approaching the end of a long career. His position in the Cape colony ends with an appointment as Deputy Adjutant-General to the army in India. There he joins the staff of Sir Hugh Gough to experience an Indian battlefield in the Gwalior War of 1843 as the power of the Marathas is finally crushed. Smith has little time for his superior's 'bull at a gate' style of battlefield tactics, but independent command is denied him. Little does he realise that the greatest opportunity of his military life is close at hand.

THE GURKHA WAR by *H. T. Prinsep*—The Anglo-Nepalese Conflict in North East India 1814-1816.

SOUND ADVANCE! by *Joseph Anderson*—Experiences of an officer of HM 50th regiment in Australia, Burma & the Gwalior war.

THE CAMPAIGN OF THE INDUS by *Thomas Holdsworth*—Experiences of a British Officer of the 2nd (Queen's Royal) Regiment in the Campaign to Place Shah Shuja on the Throne of Afghanistan 1838 - 1840.

WITH THE MADRAS EUROPEAN REGIMENT IN BURMA by *John Butler*—The Experiences of an Officer of the Honourable East India Company's Army During the First Anglo-Burmese War 1824 - 1826.

BESIEGED IN LUCKNOW by *Martin Richard Gubbins*—The Experiences of the Defender of 'Gubbins Post' before & during the sige of the residency at Lucknow, Indian Mutiny, 1857.

THE STORY OF THE GUIDES by *G.J. Younghusband*—The Exploits of the famous Indian Army Regiment from the northwest frontier 1847 - 1900.

AVAILABLE ONLINE AT
www.leonaur.com
AND OTHER GOOD BOOK STORES

www.ingramcontent.com/pod-product-compliance
Lightning Source LLC
Chambersburg PA
CBHW021004090426
42738CB00007B/652